IN
TRANSIT

IN
TRANSIT

A 365-Day Transition from the Corporate World to
You-Are-on-Your-Own-and-Good-Luck-with-That!

GISELE AUBIN

iUniverse, Inc.
Bloomington

IN TRANSIT
A 365-Day Transition from the Corporate World to
You-Are-on-Your-Own-and-Good-Luck-with-That!

iUniverse books may be ordered through booksellers or by contacting:

iUniverse
1663 Liberty Drive
Bloomington, IN 47403
www.iuniverse.com
1-800-Authors (1-800-288-4677)

Because of the dynamic nature of the Internet, any web addresses or links contained in this book may have changed since publication and may no longer be valid. The views expressed in this work are solely those of the author and do not necessarily reflect the views of the publisher, and the publisher hereby disclaims any responsibility for them.

Any people depicted in stock imagery provided by Thinkstock are models, and such images are being used for illustrative purposes only.
Certain stock imagery © Thinkstock.

ISBN: 978-1-4759-5970-3 (sc)
ISBN: 978-1-4759-5972-7 (hc)
ISBN: 978-1-4759-5971-0 (ebk)

Library of Congress Control Number: 2012921233

Printed in the United States of America

iUniverse rev. date: 12/21/2012

In praise of *In Transit*.

"*In transit* is one of those very few books that truly engages the reader. If you've ever asked yourself, "Is this all there is?" then you want to read Gisele Aubin's story about how she dramatically re-invented herself. At an age where many individuals feel that the best of their career or their personal life is now behind them, she moved forward into a successful and satisfying new life. Her story is compelling, informative and genuine. As a business life coach myself, I will recommend this book to my own clients. Anyone looking for some new ideas and a fresh perspective about how to continue life's journey will enjoy and value Gisele's book."

—John M. McKee,
Founder, The Business Success Coach Network

"In *In transit*, Gisele Aubin offers a realistic portrait of transition and what people can expect to feel and experience when they make the leap to self-employment or any other major leap in life. Instead of easy answers and step-by-step lessons, she offers her readers the freedom and opportunity to explore, reexamine, and get to know themselves again. It's a refreshing voice and a reminder that we all need to coach and coach ourselves again through life's many twists and turns and new adventures."

—Tyler R. Tichelaar, Ph.D.
and author of the award-winning Narrow Lives

DEDICATION

I dedicate this book to the memory of Antoinette, better known as Toni (1919-2012) who in her own unpretentious way, was a magic and mysterious personality in my life. She opened a window for me into a bigger world. Her generosity made many things possible, including the publishing of this book.

ACKNOWLEDGMENTS

To my siblings: Benoit who instilled in me at a very early age, the notion of capability, and rekindled it more recently in saying, "Sis, you can write!" Suzanne who read every blog I posted and every line of my book with the sharp eyes of an English teacher and saved me from multiple embarrassments and Denis who took my efforts so seriously and supported my business with genuine care.

To my partner, Andre, who put up with my anguish and endless quests for the right words, the perfect sentence, the best expression, morning day and night, and for so long.

To my colleagues and friends: M.J. Burrows, who agreed to spend part of her Cuban vacation reading and commenting on my book; Brian Blackburn, who time and time again, walked me through the marketing plan of my business and let me leave the restaurant without paying, so engrossed I was in my thoughts, and never complained. To my coach, Jan Carley, who pushed and pushed, and then when she was done, pushed some more to make me bring that book to completion. To the following individuals, who at one time or other answered my plea for their feedback on titles, pictures, design, pace, etc. and did so, generously: Tammy Harrington, James Morrison, Sophie Chambers, Patrice Laserre, Angela Newman, Harry Gaber, Judi Summerlin, Garlyn Dewar, Nina Makloski, Mike Kennedy, Judith Hageman, Mia Pak, Robert Zalaudek, Wayne Page, Carl Kumpic, Mona Attard, Diane Letourneau, Kirsten Starcher, Bruce McLeod, Reta Byvelds, Ed Catenacci, Taji Mahone, Mario Patenaude, Lora Lilli, Annette Siewertsen, Jane Hardy, Eric Pedersen, Anne Huet, Irene Barr, Ian McDonald, and I am sure I am missing some. To my former boss and mentor, Clark Handy, who in my professional life never let me down. To John McKee, who agreed to read my manuscript and endorse it in such a generous way despite his unbelievably busy schedule. To Michel Trépanier, who long before I even knew I would write a book, taught me the value of never giving up even when it would have been so tempting to do so. To George Nedeff, who was so understanding and patient with me throughout the book production process. To Tyler Tichelaar, who put on the final touch and wrapped it all nicely for me when it looked like it was falling apart.

To my children Jean-François, André Philippe, and Julie Anne, who followed my progress the way I followed their score cards at school: with neurotic interest.

Finally, to my parents Léon Aubin and Alice Roy, who have taught me the value of hard work and unconditional love. Frankly, what else is there?

To all of you, I want to express my endless gratitude and say that caring for others is the most noble activity. You are my inspiration. I will pay it forward.

PREFACE

Change is not the challenge—Transition is.

Change is an external event; the only process I know that starts with an ending.

Transition is an internal process. It is you dealing with yourself and it is a lot more difficult to define. It usually unfolds this way:

> **The ending:** An event occurs, your world as you know it comes to an end and you don't really know where to go.

> **The retreat**: A time when confusion reigns. You are nostalgic of your past, in denial of your present and clueless about your future. You need to turn inward and reconnect with yourself.

> **The ramping up:** A time of adherence and resistance when alignment starts taking place through trials and tribulations.

> **The new beginning:** When the new reality finally sets in, mostly because you have sorted things out for yourself and started making choices and embracing the new life.

It is that simple, but it is not so simple.

Change is necessary. It is healthy and can be loaded with excitement. Think of it as a wave. Learning to ride it will get you places. Resisting it will knock you over.

Which will it be?

Everything is up for grabs, and whether I land on my head or on my feet remains to be seen. I will give myself 365 days to reinvent my life, one more time. Why 365? Because change takes time and I want to do this right, and if I don't do it right, it can go on forever.

This book is not a five-step formula to fortune and fame; it is a story—my story. It has flaws, fears, fun, and an inside view of a day-to-day life when everything is subject to change. It's not all pretty, but it's real. At times, there may be more grind than glamour, but the good news is, it can be done. Changing your life that is.

If you are willing to redefine success and perhaps a few other things in your life, as may be required, then you're good to go. If you don't know how to do it, then you want to read this book.

Success is not necessarily making it onto the Who's Who list; nor is it the privilege of a few gifted or lucky ones. It is more about making your everyday life better, and working at it with whatever you've got, but with everything you've got. It happens one day at a time, more often than not, the way you least expect it, so there is no need to sweat the lack of blueprints. All you need is a beginning and an end. Don't worry about the middle. If it hadn't been said already, I would tell you, "Just do it!"

What matters is that you take the first step and get started.

———— ✦ ————

At my mid-fifties milestone, with a successful career but an exhausted mind, a tired body, a severely challenged romantic life—as I am hardly ever home—and a general feeling that things are not as good as they should be, I long for something else, something happy. I have a constant uneasy feeling hanging on to me, much like when you leave home thinking you have forgotten something, but can't quite figure out what it is. It is just not going away.

A lot is going on, but somehow, it all seems to be happening on the surface and nothing is moving me on the inside. Although I have it good by most people's standards, it is mostly bad by mine. Something has to change, and I am not sure what, or how.

Then, just when I think I have reached a dead end, my job comes to a fork in the road, and I elect to see this as an opportunity. The company I work for is sold. I have the option to stay with the new owner or leave. It all happens rather quickly, at a crazy busy time, and I do not have the luxury to stop and think about what will happen next. All I know is that I want out. Out sounds good. Loving an impulsive decision more than anything else, I elect to bail out

I transition out of the corporate world the way you leave someone at the gate when you are late for your flight—suddenly. I join the ranks of the unemployed like you enter a sauna—with anticipated relief and no intention to stay for very long. Finally, I discover entrepreneurship the way I would enter a party where I know no one—with some anxiety, looking for something or someone familiar, and wondering whether I have crashed the wrong party.

What follows is a year of relentless learning where everything is a new encounter and subject to scrutiny; is it genuine or just passing? More than anything else, there is uncertainty. Much to my surprise, the biggest piece of the puzzle is not the economy, the market conditions, the competition or any outside elements. The biggest challenge is me and how I deal with it all. And that's good news because that is the only piece I can control.

Changing your life is possible. It does not come easily, but it happens steadily. What you need is to set your mind to it, stay the course, and pull yourself up by the bootstraps.

It is possible. So much is possible.

PART I

It does not matter how many times in my life I start over. It is still a challenge. The first time was after college when I had to decide between entering the job market and pursuing my education. While contemplating career choices, the prospect of selecting *anything* for the rest of my life was daunting. Frankly, there was nothing I wanted to do for the next forty years because there was everything I wanted to explore. Choosing to bypass further schooling, I got a job within two weeks. This was the market in the late '70s. I worked for a year with the sole purpose of saving enough money to be able to quit my job. The goal was to travel. I was never able to convince my dad of that strategy. He just would not understand why I would give up such a good thing. My argument was, "Once you know there is more out there, why would you settle for less?"

So I flew to Paris on a one-way ticket and left everyone behind, including a promising young man who had to stay to complete his degree. The objective was to go out and explore, and mostly to discover the unknown because how else would I know what I didn't know?

I was on my own, experiencing an unbelievable state of equal vulnerability and freedom. I realized that they often come together. I learned about autonomy, self-reliance, stillness, the depth of one's own resources, and the incredible, indescribable richness of life when you are open to what it has to offer, whether you had planned for it, or not.

I felt capable, beautiful, and limitless. All in all, a good year.

Then, nearly a year later, this promising young man, who had stayed behind, came to fetch me. After all that time away, I fell for him again. He had no difficulty convincing me to go back. So I did. And I married him with the deepest conviction that it was the right thing to do. If ever in my life I felt grounded, solid, and convinced, it was definitely when I stood at the altar next to him and said, "I do."

Then it happened again. Starting over again, I mean, when my marriage blew up twenty years later. That time, it was not voluntarily. Of course, marriages don't blow up overnight. They erode with time. I could not see that then. I was completely lost, feeling cheated, betrayed, confused, hurt; in fact, any pain-related word you can think of can be added to this litany. It was a crisis for which I was unprepared, ill-equipped, and overwhelmed, but I had to face it just the same.

At age twenty, getting on a plane headed for Europe somehow felt like a whole lot better way to start over. It had been fun and full of promises. This time around was difficult. The only commonality between these two journeys was the need for self-sufficiency. I had relied on someone else to take care of me financially and emotionally, and now I had to backtrack and find my way to recovery. It was a struggle for quite some time until I understood that only I could change my life. Looking back, I know that coming to that realization was the kicker. A simple statement, but it was a long time coming. I figured my best way out was to get a decent career, which I did not have at the time. I had a job. My passion and vision had been in my family. But now things had changed. Family was still number one, but how I would keep it a priority would require major overhaul.

So I applied myself and started building a new reality for my children and me. In the process, I flushed everything I otherwise knew as my life. Once you start ripping away a corner of your life, you quickly realize that much like your kitchen renovation, it is very hard to make anything new out of the old stuff. I moved into a new city, a new job, a new industry, a new house, and essentially, a new life. I also changed my car; might as well. I like to say that I kept only the kids. Considering that they were fifteen, twelve, and seven, that alone was an undertaking.

As I went along, I don't think I had time to stop and think about whom I was becoming. It didn't matter. It was not the object. I was on a roll, or rather a climb; the corporate climb as it was.

Human resources was my field of expertise; leadership was my natural groove; hard work was my mantra, and as far as I was concerned, I was not going to stop until I got to the top, wherever that was. I figured a time would come when I would feel I had succeeded, and I would know when that would be. The goal was to provide for my kids and myself in a way that would offer us options in life, a sound education for them, and a happy retirement prospect for me, and hopefully, a good life in-between.

I got busy and gradually life got better. In time, I was able to enjoy the benefits of a successful career, and I expanded my role to a global scope, where until very recently, my home was in Vancouver, my office in Florida, my boss in Cincinnati, my children in Montreal, my team scattered around the world, and my best friends in Quebec City. God only knows where my boyfriend was. I was confused. Had I arrived? Was this how success was supposed to feel?

This is how I find myself in a similar place of change, again, minus the crisis. This time, the journey to change my life is intentional.

Change may be a desired state, but it is nevertheless a scary one. A great deal of anxiety surrounds it. On the inside, the doubts, the fears, the uncertainty around the decision to quit my job and change my career all contributed to creating a constantly recurring litany of questions and debates with myself, something like a deafening noise in my head, for which I had no volume control—much like being at a rock concert twenty-four hours a day. No intermission. It is not always easy. It requires a whole lot of determination and some getting used to, not to mention the ability to face your own fears head on.

I didn't have much to get started on since I didn't really have time to plan any of it. All I had was the stubborn conviction that there had to be more out there. I also had some time on my hands, and enough money stashed aside to last me until I landed on my feet, provided I was careful and didn't take too long—altogether, not such a bad start.

Even without really knowing what I was on the lookout for, I knew it had little to do with a three-car garage, Louis Vuitton, or even a romantic weekend in Paris. It was not about stuff. It did have everything to do with self, stretching and daring to move past my fears to find out how far I could go, whom I would be in the process, and of course, where I would land in the end.

My hope is that by reading the day-to-day reality of my transition year, others will associate it to their own desires for their lives and find that they too can take it a step further.

So, from this point on, it is my journey, but it could just as well be anyone else's.

———————

The eighteen months preceding the sale of our division are anything but your same old, same old scenario. They are pretty much a frantic, non-stop, survival reality show. The business is losing money beyond the definition of acceptable, the board is expecting much more from us, the leadership team, and the executive committee is irritated by our inability to turn the ship around, and our clients are squeezing us for everything we have.

Our saving grace is that the economy is in the tank and our leader is one incredibly stubborn man. We aren't going down until the sun comes up. Count on him. What is equally working for us is that as tough as conditions are at work, the employees have nowhere to go. Nobody is hiring. So we all hunker down and take the bull by the horns, bring our division from loss to profit, and sell the damn thing.

So it is more than just putting lipstick on the pig and selling it. It is about making it right.

And we do. We take what initially looks like a situation bigger than life and tackle it, one step at a time. We call it "slicing the elephant," dealing with issues, one bite size piece at a time. Make no mistake. Due diligence is not for the faint of heart. It is real hard work. It takes a village to make it happen.

While we are meeting with potential buyers, going through every twist and turn of internal data, again and again, we continue to support over three million employees and retirees around the world. We implement new systems and services, also all around the world, and do so while conducting a sweeping restructuring. We offshore a large portion of the business and downsize our North American footprint considerably.

In some areas of the world, we have to manage significant downsizing. In others, evidently, we manage growth. Instant, hurried, make-it-happen-now kind of growth. Managing growth is a lot more fun than downsizing, but no less work. Also, taking from Peter to pay Paul, as we find ourselves doing when we shut down offices in one part of the world to open them somewhere else, is not an easy thing to do. People don't always take well to surrendering their paychecks to their colleagues.

For too many of us, it has become a typical day at the office. If there is an equivalent to the Richter scale for measuring stress in the workplace, my guess is we are busting it.

My part of the deal is to manage change and lead the resources through it. Typically, change and people tend to butt heads. The first always creates friction on the latter. So friction, tension, frustrations are all additions to the already fairly loaded days. No two days are the same, but most weeks start the same way, and that is early and on all cylinders.

***

Monday morning—5 a.m. Mondays are always a hard start. My colleagues are on the East Coast for the most part and I on the West Coast. Before my day begins, I am already behind.

Every other week, I get on a plane and fly 2,800 miles diagonally across North America to spend the week at my Florida office. Sounds like a vacation destination, but it is no picnic.

When the cab to take me to the airport pulls into the driveway at 9 a.m., I have already held several calls, answered a myriad of emails, and gotten most balls in the air. My secretary makes sure I have all the day's highlights so I can work on the plane and be ready to reply when I get on the ground in Chicago for my ninety-minute connection.

Coordination is the word.

From the backseat of the cab, I return phone calls. Voicemail is a relentless 24/7 reality. I try to put out as many fires as I can before going underground, or rather above clouds, for the next four and half hours.

Juggling with a running laptop, passport, and boarding pass, while crushing my phone on my shoulder, I am often one of the last passengers to board. What is a girl to do when boarding starts before the download is completed? Efficiency is sometimes a matter of seconds . . . .

The long flights are the best. I totally zoom out from the cabin around me, and zoom in on my screen. Those four and a half hours in the air are like eight in the office. Where else do you have the luxury to be shielded from the endless phone calls, emails, instant messaging, and whatever other ways people have to reach you? The day they allow mobile phones and Internet access on all flights is going to be the day I stop commuting, I hope.

Ninety minutes on the ground in Chicago. I have my routine down pat. I welcome the endless walk from terminal B to terminal F. This is the only stretch I get all day. I love the underground walkway. The lights are subdued and so is the music. Feels like being in a cave . . . very soothing—when my phone is not ringing that is.

O'Hare has improved so much compared to earlier years. I used to think I should seriously look into getting a boyfriend in Chicago for all the nights I spent there by myself in some remote Quality Inn, or whichever hotel was available on the shuttle route. "Stranded passengers" they used to call us—the poor losers who had flown in on a late flight and missed their last connection out, on account of weather, heavy traffic, gate changes, or whatever else came up!

Had I gotten that boyfriend, the relationship would probably be but a picture on my wall now that the vast majority of flights do connect. The food has also improved. I have my favorite restaurants. I actually look forward to the usual fruit and feta cheese salad from La Tapenade at gate B4.

You know you are in serious need of a life when excitement is a tossed salad at an airport terminal.

On a good day, there is time to sit down and eat it on the spot. On a not-so-good day, I take it with me on the plane. Not everybody appreciates the smell of feta cheese, I've noticed. On a bad day, skipping the salad altogether and starving is the only option. Starvation is always better than airline food.

On any good day, though, once I have gulped my salad, I make it to the lounge, recharge my laptop battery, never mind my own, and send/receive another round of emails. That is the endless *pas de deux*. By the time I am done dealing with everyone who has his hair on fire, the day is mostly gone. Truly, this is the ongoing cycle. At least it is mine at this point. Whatever happened to the vision of a global strategic team leading the organization into best new practices? That came and went and lasted the time that it took for the ink to dry on my offer letter, or so it seems.

I am boarding again, laptop still running. Freedom is when they close the aircraft door, and I have to shut everything down.

The next leg of my journey is only two hours. I am roughly twelve hours into my day. Outside the aircraft window, it is dark already. The passengers have shifted from reading the morning paper or working on their laptops to reading Grisham or their favorite magazines. Some are sleeping. For the most part, their day is over. They are heading home.

Me? I am still on my way to work hitting the keyboard as if there is no tomorrow, going through the last wave of email downloaded in Chicago. I am mindful of the fact that my teams in Singapore, India, and the Philippines are already into their tomorrow and in need of answers to their questions of yesterday (my today) . . . There is no time zone when you work globally. There is only the here and now. Mine or theirs, it is all the same.

Landing in Florida, it is 11 p.m., but not quite so late in my body, given the three-hour time difference.

Sometimes, my luggage is delivered to the carousel; sometimes it is not. Once you have had to show up the next morning for a board meeting in your jeans and flip-flops on account of your luggage not making it on the same flight as you, you never let that happen again. Now I always travel in business attire with extra undies in my purse.

It's just the smart thing to do.

I pick up the car at the rental office and hit Highway 95 south. It's a forty-minute drive. I like the drive from the airport to the hotel. I know my way. I have my preferred radio station. With the window down, I take in the evening heat. A voluptuous moment in an otherwise gray and neutral day.

Because it is so late, no one is on the road except for the occasional trooper's car speeding by, so driving is very relaxing.

It is almost midnight, and I am nearing the hotel. I have to locate a pharmacy in search of some cosmetic apparatus since I have left my makeup bag on the ladies room counter in the Chicago airport lounge. If I were to tell my mother that I am cruising on the Interstate by myself past midnight to find a pharmacy to buy lipstick, she would think I had gone mad.

Maybe I have . . . .

By the time I get to my room, the clock is tracking time on a single digit number . . . it is late. Just about supper time in my body, and the only food around are Pringles, Aero chocolate bars, and for the health-conscious freaks, sodium-loaded crackers and crap cheese!

"Qui dort, dîne," we say in French.[1] My problem is that I neither sleep nor eat.

I unpack, hang everything up, and prepare for the next day. The wake-up call typically comes in at 3 a.m. in my body, and it is always painful.

I don't need to look for the light switch. I know this room inside out. I lie here wondering how healthy it is to think of this place as a second home. How many homes can one have before she feels like she no longer belongs anywhere?

⟹>●≪⟸

Of course, it did not start out this way. It was not intended for me to commute from Vancouver to Florida; nor was it intended that we would run into 2008 and its financial crisis and sell the division. But life happens. Between the time I joined this company and the time we decided to sell it, 2008 came and went, and as they say, the rest is history. What was intended to be an exciting global expansion initiative turned out to be a laser sharp single focus, as sharp as sensitive surgery would require, aimed at divesting ourselves from the mother ship. Not unlike a life crisis. Luckily for me, I already knew what it would take: head down, eyes on the ball, learn to breathe through clenched teeth, and don't make other plans just yet.

This roller coaster comes to an end on June 1st, and my own employment ends on September 3rd of the same year. The time in-between is to allow for a smooth transition for my successor. It is, in fact, a very busy period, with no time to prepare for my new life. Before I know it, we have come to the end of the transition period, and everything comes to a hard stop.

---

[1] Originating from the seventeenth century when people would travel by foot or horse and stay overnight in Inns. The rule was if you slept there you had to buy dinner as well . . . Nowadays, it often means that if you sleep, you will not feel the hunger pains.

I am pleased, relieved, and have mixed emotions. Mostly, I am exhausted.

I can't describe what the last day at the office is like. All I know is that by the time I get to the terminal for my last flight out, I am numb. I sit there, zombie-like, head against the wall, eyes in a daze, struggling with all the thoughts twirling in my head; I do not have to return calls, reply to emails, manage deadlines or crises, and yes, the world will survive and life will go on. I am thinking how odd it is that I have worked so hard at keeping it all together, and now I can let it all go, and it is all right.

Just like that, I have become one of the thousands of other travelers, wearing jeans and flip-flops, drinking coffee, chatting with others, and reading Grisham. It is my first encounter with anonymity; being in the moment where all that is needed is being me, now, and I am too early in the journey to know how hard I will find it going forward.

Before I start anything, though, I need a break.

PART II

Who looks outside dreams, who looks inside awakes.

Carl Jung

The first thing I need is some sleep, in fact, a lot of sleep. At the moment, both my head and my heart are under the radar. It is only now that I discover how much of an adrenaline junkie I have become. Like any other junkie, take away the fix and everything else falls apart. Wow.

First to sleep, then a vacation, and then we'll see.

Before I leave for my extended vacation in Europe, I spend a few days with my daughter Julie here in Vancouver. She is soon on her way back to Montreal, for good. I may not be saying it in so many words, but this move actually means she is leaving home. When she closes the door behind her, I will officially become an empty nester. Three strikes and I am out. She is my third and last child to leave home. Today, though, with the music playing louder than the hairdryer she is spinning around her head while talking on her hands-free phone with her friend, the thought of becoming an empty nester does not have such a bad ring to it.

We have tickets to see *Hair* tonight, the famous Broadway musical. The performance is taking place on Granville Island. The show is as I remembered it: colorful, exciting, and full of a special energy. We stay on after the show, and the entire cast comes back on stage. We talk of their hopes, aspirations, and how they all see their lives going forward. I tell them about how my life was at their age. I think it was easier than theirs, honestly.

I find I have a pretty good story to tell them, after all. I am thoroughly enjoying this interaction with the cast; it is so refreshing.

11

I am thinking that in my next job, I should try to work with younger people. They are eager, hungry, and willing to try anything. What a great attitude. Somehow, I think it requires more courage on their part to face the world today than it did for me to face mine at their age. It seems a much bigger world they are in now than the one I had to deal with.

On the way back, Julie is driving. We are still high from the music and the aura of the overall evening. We are chatting. She turns to me and asks, "Mom, when did you stop being a hippie?"

Huh? Where did that come from?

I do not remember telling her how at twenty, with an arts degree in hand and one year of traveling in Europe under my belt, I had become what you could easily refer to as a hippie. Knowing me today in my executive role and my pencil skirts and high heels, you would never think of me as a flower child in long skirts and toe cap boots. However, I was at one time, and those who know me well know some of that still lingers in me. My daughter is looking for it.

Should I?

I am quickly scanning my life backwards, trying to find out how I traded my long skirts for those pencil skirts. Did I ever make that choice, or did it just happen?

It must have gradually happened. No one forced me along the way, but frankly speaking, it does feel at times as if I have strayed from some core principles . . . . This sensation of void hanging around me might just be a testimony of that.

Before I start working on building a new life for myself, I want to make a pause. I am thinking sabbatical; a time to rest, reflect, and re-launch. I will not hurry into the next thing that comes along, but instead, seek to see what unfolds naturally.

My very first decision is to go on vacation. Vacation is a good time. It does not count against the stress of being unemployed.

Tem and I leave for France to attend my niece's wedding and then travel to Corsica.

Tem is not his real name. I call him so as he is "The Exceptional Man" in my life now. He lives in Montreal, and I, in Vancouver. Not much in my life is simple. He is part of the equation and one of the elements that tipped the balance in favor of a new life. Despite his being indeed exceptional, my track record so far would have me rating high on the scale of relationship meltdown—not because of any wrongdoing on his part, but rather because of my inclination to keep running away. Working globally allows you to dodge any commitment requirement and feel justified for doing so.

No more so. My life is looking at me, square in the face.

My first leg is a flight to Montreal where I meet Tem, and from there, drive to La Malbaie on the St. Lawrence River's north shore, east of Quebec City. We spend a few days in a place where peace and beauty rule. We both need to come down a few notches and slow the speed of our crazy lives before we can strap ourselves on an aircraft seat for an overseas flight.

Four days later, we board the plane to Nice, France. It is early in the afternoon when we land. We are jet-lagged all day, but resist going to bed now so we can give in early in the evening. We sleep fifteen hours straight before waking up late, very late, to pick up my other niece (also flying in from Montreal for the wedding) at the airport. She had a tight connection in Paris, and had she missed it, we would not have been able to wait for her before leaving for Italy. She had been warned and was nervous about being left behind. We may be on a vacation, but we are, unfortunately, on a tight schedule at first. Be there or else. Now she lands, thrilled to be here on time, and no one is there to greet her. She is thinking that we have left already.

Obviously, the four days in La Malbaie have not sufficed to rest our bodies adequately. With our missed wake-up call and the confusion of going to the wrong terminal, we finally find her with more than one hour delay. Sigh of relief. We are then off to Parma, Italy, to pick up my son Philippe, who has been there for the last four months finishing a culinary degree. If the wonderful espresso that Italy is notorious for was not enough to keep us awake, the scenic road and the unique Italian driving style were. Our ability to drive on narrow roads has changed forever, and so, I must admit, have the bumpers on the car we were driving!

As we pull into the residence's courtyard where Philippe lives and works, I spot him, standing tall, looking slender, elegantly leaning against the stone wall, smiling broadly at us. I have missed him. I close my eyes and see his dad some thirty years ago. After all has been said and done, it is still a nice picture.

He takes us on a tour of the facilities—an old castle, inside of which is a Relais et Chateaux restaurant. We are shown to our room, which appears to be straight out of a movie set. I am half-expecting King Umberto of the House of Savoy to ride in on his horse. This place is something else. I am quite impressed—and even more so by how nicely my son has picked up Italian as a third language. What a seductive language.

The owner is our host for the evening. Champagne is served on the terrace overlooking the fields, where the fowls and cattle share the day. The meal is spectacular and equaled only by the service. Above all, it is incredible to be here with loved ones. I feel I have been beamed up into another life.

My niece has been up for twenty-six hours solid, but holding up. However, dessert and a nightcap do her in. It is well past midnight by the time we drop her at the pension in the village and make our way back to the castle.

The next day, we head back to the French Riviera after a copious breakfast. The wedding is in Mougins, perched in the hills overlooking the Mediterranean, one hour drive from Nice, in a breathtakingly beautiful location.

The ceremony is outdoors, at the foot of centennial trees where the eucalyptus scent blends perfectly with the aroma of rose petals scattered on the ground. Cocktails are served on the terrace overlooking the gardens. The crowd is sophisticated, the caterer outstanding, and the day, one of great festivity.

Finally, two days later, Tem and I bid farewell to everyone and board the ferry to Corsica, where we will spend time touring the island and reconnecting with each other.

Two weeks of sunshine, fresh air, resting, dining and wining late into the night: So far, unemployment is bliss!

Lurking in the back of my mind, though, as we near the end of our stay, is the very pressing reality that a crossroad is fast approaching. What will I do when I return? What will I find? Where will it lead?

These are questions I will ask myself, time and time again, in the next 365 days.

PART III

*Everyone thinks of changing the world. No
one thinks of changing himself.*

Leo Tolstoy

In every meeting I ever attended, every presentation I ever made,
every project I ever introduced, a details-focused freak was always in the
group. Instead of listening to what was being said, he was typically busy
looking for flaws in what was being presented. So if my carried-over
balance did not match the previous month on account of a missing
dot, or a typo, I could count on him to point it out, on the spot. I
have grown accustomed to such people. I know one is in every crowd.
So, for the record, and for my own goal-tracking purposes, my new
life starts here. Anything I tag with a timeline starts here, and it may
not add up, precisely, to 365 days. It stretches out a bit, but it doesn't
matter, and you have been warned.

Wednesday, September 8

I am back home in Vancouver. And already unsure that I like my
new life. I am jet-lagged. The clock shows 3:15 a.m. Amazing how
empty an empty apartment feels in the middle of the night. Even the
city is quiet. The urge to "do" something—to have a plan, to turn my
BlackBerry on, to check my agenda—is already eating away at me.
I need somebody to need something from me. It is like poison ivy
itching away at my skin. I have an urge.

So soon?

15

I go through a whole month's mail that accumulated while I was away. It gives me the opportunity to create a "To Do" list. Insurance to renew, bills to pay, appointments to make. It feels better already.

The real elephant in the room though is the piece of porcelain that is no longer here; my daughter. This, more than the job going away, is what is weighing on me. As much as I have dreamed of the time when my life would be entirely my own again, I am disturbed by what this means.

Thirty-plus years of mothering has come to an end: a second nature needs to shift and find its way.

Shift to what, though? Taking care of houseplants is just not the same. It will take more than that. In reality, I am fighting the urge to want to take care of anything. I am not sure it is healthy to seek to be something or someone else's mother at this point. What if I just take care of me? It sounds great, but it feels uncomfortable.

Why is that? It seems to me that I should feel liberated. Am I?

Patience is a virtue that I don't know I will ever acquire, I confess. So, my impatient self wants to face this change head-on and get it over with, and even though I said I can take whatever time it takes, I want to see my future settled now. Man! It sure did not take me long to fast forward this into a potential mess.

To help me deal with this discomfort around the unknown, I do as I have always done when facing confusion; rearrange my closets as though they are my life.

In the process, I need to call Julie. So much of her is still in here. We go over the clothes she left behind to figure out what I can get rid of and what I should keep.

"What about the green gym bag?" I ask.

"You can throw it away," she says. Okay, good. This is a good start. I feel efficient and it is good. "And your grade five gymnastics suit?"

"Keep it!"

"Really?" At her age, I bet it would still fit her. I can remember wearing skirts at forty that I used to wear at twenty. Those days are gone now. Today, I am lucky if what I bought last spring still fits . . . .

"Your beat-up, stained, stuffed teddy bear?"

"Mom! You can't get rid of that!"

"Honey, you'd be surprised what I can do!"

This process is going to be an exercise in negotiation. I can tell. It actually feels good, particularly getting rid of the empty boxes she was collecting and piling up in her closet while I was storing my winter clothes in bags under my bed. Square footage is a scarce commodity in Vancouver! To retrieve some of it makes me feel rich.

Getting rid of excess items, putting her life away in boxes, removing her books from my desk—these are all ways of claiming my space back and making sure I start right away occupying it. That time of my life when I had to share everything has come and gone.

I am starting to get the hang of it.

Thursday September 9

While still employed, I had joined a by-invitation-only, executive forum group in Vancouver. The CEO and chairperson of the group had invited me for lunch at a prestigious private club here downtown. Of course, I was impressed with the venue, but mostly, as I listened to her explaining what the forums were all about—namely a place where executives get together to discuss challenges and issues they have at work, where they can find peer support away from the workplace's internal competition, and be with individuals who have no agenda other than being part of the group—I was impressed with her job, and I told her so.

I think I startled her. "I do love it actually; it is a great job," she eventually said. I sure thought so. I wondered whether I could ever be in a place where my job would bring me such satisfaction and pleasure.

If ever someday, someone asks me to describe my dream job, I will describe hers.

So now, I am unemployed, but I am still part of the forum, at least until my membership runs out in a few months. Today is our first meeting following the summer break. I am not sure how it will go. The thought of walking into that meeting, unemployed, feels like this dream where you get on the bus naked and hope nobody will notice. Uncomfortable is an understatement.

I'm not too sure why I feel that way. Perhaps we just won't seem to be in the same place—the other members and I. However, I don't let that stop me. In fact, I am so happy to have an opportunity to dress up, work with a schedule, and review the agenda that I would not miss this meeting for the world.

Old habits dic hard!

I leave my condo a bit early, and on my way, stop to renew my home insurance. That is definitely a perk of being unemployed; taking care of the day-to-day stuff in a timely and easy manner as opposed to packing it all on your weekends. The clerk hands me the forms to complete. I come across a novelty.

"Your business address?" he asks. I freeze. It is unthinkable for me to say that I no longer have a job. I feel the need to explain.

"I work from home, but I was in Florida; now I am back, but I am no longer working . . . but . . . ."

Blank stare. "Just the address," he repeats.

Of course. He doesn't care. He just wants me to fill in the boxes. I could write my dentist's address for all he knows. I need to get over this awkward feeling—it actually feels like the first time someone called home for my husband after he moved out. Why I didn't think of just saying, "He no longer lives here" is beyond me today, but at the time, it seemed insurmountable.

At the meeting, I hear talks of deadlines, profit & loss statements, downsizing, etc., and an overwhelming nauseous feeling hits me. I blame it on being jet-lagged, but I know better. As of now, I don't want to re-enter this business world. I was happy in it for a good number of years, but now, somehow, it leaves me hanging. It is as if all the lights have been turned off and everything around me is flat.

I guess thinking that way can be considered "normal" on day two of what is intended to be a sabbatical.

However, all kinds of guilt enter my mind. Then fear creeps in. Will I think this way for the rest of my life? If I don't want to dwell in this environment anymore, then surely welfare is my only alternative. What else is there for me?

Of course, I think in terms of all or nothing: Always. Black and white. There is abundance, and then there is scarcity. The place in-between is never familiar ground for me, and I have a nagging suspicion that this place in-between is what I will need to get acquainted with in the months ahead.

Thinking in black-and-white terms, I suspect, is nothing but cowardice in disguise. As long as I keep telling myself that my only options are killing myself on the job or showing up at the soup line, I give myself permission to stall. So, black and white is where I hide.

I share my awkwardness with my colleagues on the forum. My mood swings between wanting to pursue a successful career and the desire to plant a garden and watch it grow, day-in and day-out. I don't seem to have anywhere to go in-between.

Their words are comforting. Mostly, the message is "Give yourself time; take this one day at a time, and let it come."

Give yourself time actually sounds like a gift. Not being pressured and cornered to deliver is such a novelty. For a brief moment, I feel the voluptuous sensation of time and what it is like to have plenty of it.

I feel high as I leave. To let it come also has a sweet ring to it. I like that. Life happens. You don't make it. You take it.

Many argue the opposite, particularly in the professional arena where we are taught to work with goals, objectives, a ninety-day, annual, and five-year plan, where you never leave anything unplanned. If anyone still believes that you can plan and control everything in your daily life, then I suggest you babysit your brother's kid for a weekend or get a new boss overnight. You'll see what I mean.

This business of planning is something I need to mention. The child I was while growing up, the young adult I became, the now older, presumably wiser, grown-up that I am, hates planning. There I said it. It is as counterintuitive to me as it is for a mother bear to let strangers come near her cubs. It is just not in my nature. If I had my way, I would get up every morning and decide, then-and-there, what the day will bring. However, I had to learn to plan. I would not have survived in the business world otherwise. So planning is a necessity. I get it. Totally. But I reserve the right to avoid it every time I can.

I leave the group in a much better mood than when I arrived. On the way home, I stop and buy dinner at Capers—the local health food takeout store. Depending on takeout has become a habit of mine. For three reasons, I want to break that habit: 1) cost, 2) my waistline, and 3) guilt. I come from a family where the only thing we bought at the grocery store was meat (non-processed) and dairy. My mom made everything else; a tough act to follow, and yet I did for a while. To think that once I baked my own bread, made my own yogurt and granola cookies, not to mention upside-down lemon cake!

Surely, mastering the art of French cooking as Julia Child would have it will come back, but for now, food for survival is the level I am at. It will come back. No worries. There is time.

Heading out with my dinner neatly wrapped in a brown paper bag, I hear my phone ring. It's a wrong number, but it serves as a reminder that I need to return the office equipment assigned to me by my former employer—my BlackBerry and laptop; my two lifelines. I have held onto them long enough. To ship them back in a box and walk away from the FedEx office will be similar to dropping your firstborn child at day-care on day one of going back to work. A serious dose of insecurity is wrapped around it.

So that means I need another phone, and another laptop.

Sigh.

I do not like shopping. It tires me instantly. No matter what I shop for (except perhaps shoes and jewelry), I find the choice to be simply too vast—even when reading the menu in restaurants; I am happy when someone recommends a selection so I can skip that part.

I am not lazy. Just a tad impatient! So I decide to ask a friend to help me. I need someone to shield me from myself when it comes to shopping.

She gracefully agrees. "Call me when you are ready," she says.

I feel better already.

Saturday, September 11

Saturday morning. Today does not feel any different than all the Saturdays when I was working, except there is no need for me to review any leftover files from the week before, finish any reports, or prepare any meetings for next week. My desk is clear. Somehow, I can breathe better.

I love mornings. I swear to myself that no matter what I do in the future, I will protect my mornings. They are the guardian of my sanity. To start the day on all cylinders is not how I want to be going forward. Note to self and everybody else. Don't mess with my mornings!

Mornings can easily stretch to noon if I am left alone. These days, that is exactly what happens. I am left alone. In fact, there is no reference to anything. I can get up, eat, read, sleep, go out and stay out for as long as I want. I don't even have to come home. I have no obligations.

Imagine that.

For all the times in my life when I traded what I wanted to do with what I had to do, I thought it would feel better to reach this stage when no one or nothing needs my attention. But there is a bit of a No Man's Land feeling to it . . . . like an echo that keeps coming back, or a void somewhere wanting to be filled. I have enough sense to know that danger lies in filling it with the first thing that comes along, but not enough wisdom to know what to fill it with. All I know is that anxiety exists around it that I had not anticipated. That's for sure.

So, to beat the blues, I continue my clean-up job in Julie's bedroom and every part of the condo that she claimed as hers. De-cluttering and rearranging my physical space gives me the illusion that I am actually doing the same for my mental space. It is hugely therapeutic.

In the process, I come across some camping gear in my car trunk, partially deflated air mattresses in the basement locker, and dirty beddings in the laundry basket . . . not to mention size 11 men's tennis shoes. Somehow, because I know these items are the last remnants of Julie's busy life in Vancouver, I don't mind. I will clean up. One last round for old time's sake!

However, I can only stand crawling under beds and shuffling clothes for so long. As planned, I meet my girlfriend downtown. We go through my mobile phone strategy and shopping need. I work best when I can bounce ideas off someone. She is most helpful. In the end, because a new iPhone is coming out at the end of the month and new promotions will take place, her best advice is to wait a little bit longer.

Legitimate procrastination—I couldn't have asked for anything better.

As for any good shopping, we end up at the bar. Sometimes I love shopping.

Sunday, September 12

Sundays are different. I need to leave my friends alone. Most of them are in relationships. So am I, but mine comes with a 3,000 miles caveat. We don't spend all our Sundays together.

I typically visit with friends one-on-one during the week when we go for coffee, lunch, or happy hour. On Sundays, however, I don't bother them. So, I am on my own. I need to go out and play. No errands, housework, worries, or anxiety build-up in preparation for the week ahead; just fun, and now, for the first time in a long, long time, I can indulge.

I also think I need to get serious with my eating patterns—get back to cooking and try to lose those extra pounds that snuck up on me between flights and hotel stays. Already, I am drifting away from fun. Can you tell?

How I conclude that the best activity is to start with cooking a low sugar jam, I am not sure. Sometimes, I suspect that anything to take the fun away is my way to sustain the anxiety build-up I keep dealing with. The human brain is afflicted with muscle memory just like the body. Wanting to go back to the familiar state, regardless of how unpleasant or unhealthy it is, is as natural as sunrise and sunset. The battle is internal. I am beginning to figure this out. In any case, since cooking jam is the selected activity, I go online, looking for recipes, but digress to mountain climbing, house renovation, and language training sites.

I was never diagnosed with ADD, but perhaps I never had a good doctor! I am going around in circles. What to do with myself when I can do everything I want?

In the end, I never get around to cooking that jam. Being that it is Sunday, I call my Mom, Tem, my kids, and my sister, and before I know, 3 p.m. has arrived. I am still in my PJ's, and the sun has turned into rain.

Panic. Is this what my life is going to be like? Much ado about nothing?

Must I always spoil everything with something to worry about? I remind myself that it is a lazy Sunday. It is okay. I am entitled to being lazy.

Since being busy is the preferred state (heaven forbid that I should just sit and read a book), I elect to go out for a walk. A walk actually sounds pretty benign considering how I used to be at the gym religiously four to five times a week when my life was unfolding at the speed of light. I can't remember when I started slipping away from that routine, but now it is out of sight for sure.

I head out for the sea wall and end up just going around the lagoon and through Stanley Park to English Bay. A much shorter walk. My energy level simply is not back.

No sense pretending otherwise.

I head back home. Defeated, I pour myself a glass of wine, sink into my favorite armchair, and finally pick up my book where I left it. Surrender is underrated. It feels great.

Whose idea was it to go to the gym anyway?

I love Sundays when there is no Monday.

Monday September 13

Oh, the glorious mornings of not setting the alarm clock, of drinking coffee and reading the morning papers until even the obituaries have been read from top to bottom. I will never tire of that.

I need to take the car in for inspection today before renewing the insurance on it. It feels good to have an item on my agenda. So I shower and dress with a purpose; I can't help but notice how good that feels.

I leisurely drive to the garage at a time when traffic has died and all commuters are locked into their downtown towers. I pull into the entrance where the sign says there is an eight-minute wait. "We apologize for the inconvenience," it says.

They must be joking. Eight minutes are a joy. I am used to fighting crowds at lunch hour or early evenings when the waiting period was counted in hours, not minutes. So I drive in, drop the car, walk to the waiting room, buy myself a cup of coffee, sit down, and pull out my book.

No sooner have I retrieved the marker from my book than they are calling me on the speaker. The inspection is done. I can go now.

Go now? Why? I thought this task would book most of my morning? I am actually disappointed that it did not take longer. Then I feel totally confused for thinking that way. This can't be me! Frustrated because of a quick service delivery?

What is happening to me? I stand here alone between these glass walls where all I see are run-down cars, and all I hear are noisy mufflers. Nothing is familiar here. It is not even 10 a.m. and my daily tasks are all marked off. I feel guilty, useless, and mostly foolish. I feel utterly out of place. I look around for someone to understand, or better yet, to explain what is happening to me. There is no one. That makes it worse. Evidently, the rest of the world is busy leading meaningful lives while I stand here, going through what should be a totally mundane activity that has now turned into a life crisis. I am ashamed of how fragile I am. These feelings are escalating faster than I can control them. No way that they will take over my day.

I shake off these thoughts the way a dog shakes water off its back. Pick yourself up, girl.

Because I have time to spare, I stop at the car wash. A clean car would be nice. Having a clean car interior is on the list of things I have wanted to have all my life, it seems. What can I say? Not all dreams are made of gold. Normally, my car was my daughter's to use, and therefore, hers to clean as well. No free rides in this world, particularly in my car! But now she is gone. Plan B would be to take the car to the cleaners, but I decide to make a genuine effort to do things differently. Instead of buying everything, I want to see to what extent I can provide for myself in this new life I have just embarked on. So I take five bucks, ask for change, and start pumping the vacuum cleaner with coins, and begin cleaning.

Almost immediately, the hose breaks and the nozzle comes loose. I spend the remainder of my dollar trying to adjust it. I ask the attendant whether he can fix it, but he can't. I ask for a refund, but he won't give me one.

An immediate mood shift occurs, pulling me into an ugly place. I catch myself. This is just a car wash, and it is just a dollar. I can do this.

So I move the car to the next stall and ask for more change.

One thing I noticed is how volatile my temper has become. I have totally run out of patience for any of life's little hurdles such as traffic, store hours, line-ups, spilled coffee, etc.

I had to admit this volatility when, as a pedestrian, crossing the street on MY green light recently, a car zoomed by and the driver yelled at me for being on the street. I reacted with an overdose of built-up stress and literally hit his car with my fist, shouting words at him I would not want my children to hear!

Imagine that. I had become this crazy person willing to pick a street fight. To know me is to know that reaction is totally out of character.

It is what happens when you deny yourself too much in some areas of your life such as rest, contentment, recognition, etc. It pops out somewhere else under different forms, such as aggressiveness, alcohol abuse, or sickness, and it is often difficult to link the two together. Connecting the dots is not always easy.

Of course, had the driver come out of his car, I had nowhere to go! A scary thought judging by the size of him. The amusing part is, given my life now, I would not have to explain the broken nose to my boss or children since all are remarkably absent in my life these days.

So, still at the car wash, the next twenty minutes are on my hands and knees, pulling on the hose, going around doors, scraping the floor, picking out long red hair (hers), gum wrappers (his), old receipts (mine), and assorted flies and bugs. I am hot, sweaty, uncomfortable, and feel silly resisting spending thirty bucks to have someone else do it. Why bother?

Well, it is all part of my new life, or so I think. Besides, I have time. Isn't time the trade-off for money?

I make it back home with time to spare. Amazing how much time there is in a day. I head out to the sea wall, but my walk takes me to the Vancouver Aquatic Centre instead: opposite direction. You never know where your feet will take you when the head is not paying attention.

The swimmers are training. Diving lessons are taking place. As a child, I always wanted to take diving lessons, but I never did.

I stand there, taking in the chlorine smell, and listening to the echoed sounds of the pool. Maybe I should take diving lessons now. Isn't that what my sabbatical should be about? Catching up on all those lost opportunities? Trying to find the one thing that will change my life? Making it all exciting and fulfilling? I look around. The oldest student I see is probably fourteen at best! Me at the end of the diving board; that would be a sight! I am thinking that belly dancing would probably be more appropriate. At the very least, it might improve my waistline.

I head back home. Before turning in for the night, I call Tem. He is in Montreal. I am in Vancouver. We have known each other for seven years and have been in and out of a relationship for the better part of those years. He truly is an exceptional man, and among all the things he is for me, he is an incredible sounding board.

So I call him. I am struggling with my need to be productive and purposeful at the same time as my desire to be idle and find time for all the things I want in my life. How to balance it all? How long will I struggle with it?

He always helps me find the middle. "This time out will help you figure it out," he says. "You don't need to have the answer now. You don't need to do anything. In fact, you don't need anything. Give yourself time; don't be so anxious and so impatient."

Why does everybody keep telling me the same thing?

Tuesday, September 14

As the days progress, I am unsure how I feel. I will either get comfortable with this new pace and this opportunity to explore stillness and reflect, or I will grow increasingly uncomfortable. The jury is not yet out.

My biggest challenge is my mind. It is difficult to shut it off. It is racing ahead of me all the time. This internal activity may be a birth defect, I fear. I was born without an on/off switch to my brain.

At work, I was constantly facing decisions and new scenarios requiring immediate action. Constant motion. Now I think my brain is suffering from severe withdrawal. I just don't feed it as much stuff.

Seriously, I am of the opinion that my mind needs to grow up. It still acts like a kid in a candy store. It wants everything and bounces up and down in anticipation, but will not be still long enough to take in anything. I say this despite having successfully raised three children and managed a career. At times, my brain is able to behave. In other words, I can focus and deliver when I have to. Those are the key words: when I have to. At the moment, I don't "have to" anything. I don't have to provide for my children, to work for a living (for a little while at least), to deliver at work, to get dressed in the morning, to answer the phone. Heck, I don't even have to come home at night. I can do what I want. That is why my brain goes AWOL and wants to do everything.

Think of my thoughts as spilled marbles on a cement floor. See them bounce?

What will I do with my sabbatical?

Wednesday, September 15

The plan today is to update my resume and forward it to the executive recruiting firm that advertised the incredible job I saw in the paper yesterday.

Yes, I know. I said I would not do that. I would not bounce back and apply for the first job that comes along. Then I said I would not even consider a job or doing anything job-related (including updating my resume) before the New Year (at least four months away).

Well then? Well, because I got so excited reading that ad, I think it is worth exploring what is in there for me. Sometimes you have to allow your plans to be changed and accept going off course just a little bit. I have to believe this advice to be true; at least, I desperately want to.

A perfect display of brain muscle memory I'd say. In actual fact, it is a diversion. A sign of my brain desperately wanting to go back to the place it is familiar with and that is work, hard work, doing what I know best because nothing else can possibly allow me to make a living, and let's face it, everybody needs to make a living. It's hard when your worst enemy resides within you. How do you outsmart it?

This job would even mean moving east. Anyone who knows me knows that I totally love Vancouver; I would trade many things in my life before I would trade this city for another one. But somehow, this ad does it for me.

So today I want to go ahead with applying for the job, but as I sit down and look for the ad, I cannot find it anymore. I actually think I put it in the recycling bin and took everything down to the dumpster last night.

How Freudian is that?

I think this is a perfect display of my inner battle. The drive for a new life and the battle to go back to familiar surroundings. A real mental tug-of-war.

I am desperately searching for that piece of paper, but mostly, I am struggling with the decision. Shall I go ahead with this or not? Is losing the ad a sign that I should not pursue it? What would my horoscope say? Should I pull my Ouija board out? I mean I am confused here. I don't seem to be able to direct my thoughts as clearly as I used to.

When you have no certainties, the slightest little thing makes you waiver.

Seriously, all this thinking about what I want to do, how I should do it, what is right for me, what is not, is downright unnerving. My long-time friend here in Vancouver would tell me it is time to go outside and play. Good advice. I am putting my walking shoes on, grabbing my iPod, and heading out.

Two hours of fresh air and open space ought to do me some good.

Thursday, September 16

Being outdoors rested my body, but it did not clear my mind altogether. I am back at updating my resume.

I had almost given up on this project when I met a group of people on the seawall yesterday who were visiting from out of town. "Where are you all from?" I asked as I was getting ready to leave them. Wouldn't you know? They are from the very city where that job is. I take this as my cue. Once back home, I go online, look for the ad, and find it. I am determined to do this, so I proceed with the application. I hit "send" and turn off the computer, never to hear from anyone again.

At the time of sending it in, I do not know that it will lead nowhere, of course. It does not matter; what is important is that the process begins. Some wheels are in motion.

So, another item is checked off my list. I am starting to like this! I am actually beginning to understand the true benefits of "getting started." It does create momentum, a kind of motion that sucks you into doing more . . . . It is like everything else you start and build into your routine. Before long, it has become a part of your normal life, and you can deal with it.

Just like having a full-time job, night classes, three kids and a dog, no cleaning lady, and still, making it all work. Waiting until all things are figured out means never starting. Same kind of stuff.

Okay. Next. Now what? Well, I am thinking of the article in this morning's paper about a woman who took her inheritance money and embarked on a fifty country tour. Upon her return, she wrote a book on her journey and self-published it.

Wow!

It is not the journey or the article in the *Globe* that caught my attention as much as the self-publishing part. I did not know you could do that! (I am learning that there are a lot of things I don't know). Discovering things creates all kinds of possibilities. One of them for me at this stage is the option of packing everything up and hitting the road, just like she did. I did that once when I was twenty and came back a year later with the feeling of an unfinished job.

I came back because my life was calling me home. My life then was that handsome twenty-two-year-old undergrad getting ready to pack up his gear and move west to start his military training. That was his life, and I felt strongly that mine was attached to his. I did not know then that I could have my own life, and I didn't want to be left behind.

Now, thirty-five years later, I could pick up from where I left off. I have the time, money, and the same freedom from responsibilities. Here is something else to feed my frantic brain. The poor thing. I am worried that it may not survive this sabbatical.

They say there is such a thing as too much of a good thing. I shall see.

Ed is a good friend of mine here in Vancouver. Regularly, he and I meet for drinks and gossip. Neither one of us is prone to booking ahead. We often call on the spur of the moment. Works for us. We meet for what we now refer to as "Wings"—hot wings and wine.

We update each other on the latest business stories. Ed is bright, witty, and very knowledgeable on a myriad of topics. Tonight, of course, I share my thoughts about this sabbatical, my plans, my hopes, my discomfort, etc. I am seeking his opinion since I trust his judgment.

I don't easily confide in people. I don't like the idea of individuals entering the privacy of my life, but I am making an effort here. I cannot start a new life without getting out of the old one's shell. I know that most opportunities lie outside of the comfort zone. That is a given.

So I share with him my very embryonic thoughts about starting my own business, for lack of the right job existing out there, combined with a certain level of reluctance in going back to the corporate world. I also say that, technically, I should not even be thinking or talking about work at all. I am on sabbatical. However, the ability to be happy in the here and now, without knowing what tomorrow will be, is just not there for me. I can go without food today if I know there will be some in the fridge tomorrow. The reverse is not true. I simply cannot indulge today and empty the fridge, not knowing whether there will be more tomorrow. It's just my nature.

Ed not only has an opinion on my next computer selection, the best Internet provider, the best mobile phone plans, and the smartest way to set up a business, but he also offers suggestions on market niche, business partnering, potential contacts, etc. He makes it sound exciting.

My head is pleasantly spinning as I leave the restaurant. It has been a long time since I saw so many possibilities ahead of me.

The best part is that I have time to think about it, and hopefully, come up with the right decisions. So many options, so many possibilities—not the least of which is the possibility of blowing it all to hell as well! I am vibrantly aware of that. Somehow, I have this sense of a "last call" where I feel this next stretch of my professional life has to be right. I don't want to spend any time doing something I do not like, or engage in a financial downward spiral, or work with people I do not appreciate.

I am working from a clean slate here, and I am going in with an attitude. Why not make it anything I want?

Friday September 17

I have a 9 a.m. weightlifting class this morning, but can't face the thought of rushing out the door this early. I registered for that class a few weeks ago with all the eagerness of someone wanting to start a new life. I took such classes before and really liked them, but of course, as with many things in my life then, I had to drop them for lack of time and consistency. I was forever missing every other class. So between the time I registered and the time I need to show up at the door today, it would appear I've had a bit of a mind-shift. I am beginning to understand that I don't need to book my day block-to-block, and if I do, it does not need to start so early. Change is already happening. This is good.

How smoothly I deal with frustration will be my gauge for when I am ready to go back to work. At the moment, on a scale of one to ten, that ability feels somewhere around-40! And when I say frustration, I mean anything I don't feel like doing. I think this gauge is legitimate.

I am not playing princess here. I am just tired and in need of a break. Running on adrenaline and overdrive for too long will do that to you.

So today, I can safely declare that I am a long shot from being ready to deal with frustrations. I call to cancel my class. After all, I will be in Montreal for two of the next five classes. What is the point?

It turns out that the class is not until Tuesday. Really? I am almost disappointed. No reason to cancel then. So I will try again on Tuesday; see whether 9 a.m. feels better then.

It is now after lunch, and I am heading to the airport. I have a 3 p.m. flight to Kelowna, in the Okanagan Valley, the interior of British Columbia. I am visiting with my sister. She is not even one hour away by air, and in three years of promising to go up "one of these weekends," I have never got around to it. So, I am thinking I will start my sabbatical by making right by her.

Kelowna is an outdoor paradise, and as if that were not enough, it is wine country. However, this weekend it is raining. No matter. We spend a lazy weekend, talking, reading, sleeping, going to the gym to cancel out some of the wine we enjoyed earlier in the day. She is an empty nester, just like me. Her employment just ended, voluntarily, as well. She is contemplating retirement. I don't know what I am contemplating. The days unfold lazily. We shoot the breeze, which is a definite improvement from the days when we thought we would shoot each other!

Sunday September 19

I take the late afternoon flight back. Even though no one is waiting for me at the condo, it is always a thrill to return. I love my place in Vancouver so much. Mostly, I love my space.

One upside of being an empty nester is that food is still in the refrigerator when you return. The laundry basket has remained empty. The place is still tidy, and the bonus is that you are actually able to open the front door since no shoes have piled up behind it.

A novelty!

I call Mom. Because my dad is hard of hearing, I converse with him over the net. He has picked up web-based communication in his late eighties; there is a man who stretched out of his comfort zone. It is a wonderful way to stay in touch. But my mom still wants to talk. She wants to know how our weekend went.

My mom and dad are both eighty-nine years old this year. They met, were engaged, and married within six months of first laying eyes on each other. Ten months later, the first of their four children was born. It was love at first sight, and today, sixty-three years later, they still celebrate their wedding anniversary.

Their children, on the other hand, have all failed at their marriages—all four of us. Go figure! It is not as if we did not know how it should work.

My failed marriage has hung over my head as the dark cloud in my life for many years. A sense of having cheated my children out of what they deserved. As my daughter so wisely said when I was stressing over that, "Mom, don't sweat it. Where you had a pattern to follow, we will be free to make it anything we want. We don't have to try to color within the lines . . . . There are no lines. It will be easier for us than it was for you."

You gotta love her! How liberating is that? Years of agonizing over my divorce, and she whips up this answer as she maneuvers her way through traffic. Seen that way, it appears that one of my greatest life crises suddenly went from a hurricane to a breeze.

Whatever.

Monday September 20

I need to face this day. I can no longer push it back. I am getting on a plane next Saturday, and will be gone for two weeks. My equipment, namely computer and BlackBerry, need to be replaced today.

A healthy breakfast, strong coffee to get me just sufficiently on edge, comfortable shoes and clothes, sunglasses in case it becomes sunny, an umbrella (this is Vancouver) in case it rains, and extra food in my bag in case I get hungry. I take a deep breath, gather all my courage, and press the elevator button.

Coming down and heading out!

I am going shopping and need to come home with: a laptop, a mobile phone, an Internet stick, and all related software, maintenance plans, guarantee plans, etc. If you knew me, you would know this is a gigantic task. I hate this. I would rather go to the dentist.

The delta from the cheapest to the most expensive equipment is so wide you think there must be a truckload of unnecessary features, or else, a world of significant differences for sure. Without obtaining a Ph.D. in computer sciences, you want, at a minimum, to understand what you are buying. Equally, you want to know what you are opting out of. This whole process takes time and far more interest in the minutia than I will ever have. Too many options.

I will spare you the details, but I come home five hours later with all items crossed off my list. I even have some added bonuses on that list such as glossy lipsticks, a cashmere sweater, today's paper, and of course, dinner. Take out, I must confess.

The nice thing about Vancouver is that you can take out healthy food—helps to reduce the guilty feeling.

It is, however, day twelve of my sabbatical and my fridge is still empty. I do plan to pick up cooking again. Have I mentioned this?

I get home, make myself a cup of tea, sit on the balcony, and put my feet up.

I am so proud of my accomplishment today. I did not even get upset once. In fact, the personnel were quite pleasant, and I almost enjoyed myself. I learned a lot, and best of all, I am all done. I don't need to go back tomorrow.

Other than dinner, which I need, I leave everything else in the bag. It was one thing to buy all of this; it is another to set it all up.

I draw the line.

Tuesday September 21

Remember my Friday weightlifting class that got rescheduled to Tuesday? Well, this is Tuesday. I have not matured a whole lot since. I call and cancel. Nothing will get me out of the house by 8:30 a.m. Not then, not now.

What was I thinking when I booked that class? Must have been one of those days when I was on overdrive. Besides, I still have too much to do.

What are the things you think I might "have to" do while on sabbatical?

Well, for starters, set up my new computer and new mobile phone. Update all my contacts with my new data info. Set up my home files to track my business expenses (since I am thinking of going into consulting). Decide which associations, groups, or forums I should belong to. Which training or professional development I should pursue. Make up my mind (and that is no small task) whether I want to keep my frequent flyer status and commit to what it takes (time and money mostly). Identify the friends I have neglected over the years with whom I want to reconnect. Book my medical exam, mammogram, financial planner and other long neglected professionals I should see regularly. Establish a fitness program and stick to it. Dust off that piano, which has not had much of my attention, and get back to those scales. Pull out those bestsellers I have been piling up and start making my way down. Surf the local papers to make sure I capture all the events and exhibits I always invariably missed but wanted to see. Work yoga back into my schedule. Did I mention, identify a worthy cause to volunteer for? And, of course, pick up cooking again. Just to name a few.

So when I am awake at four and want to get up and get started, it is on account of all those things twirling in my head.

Honestly, I suspect all that noise and busyness to be nothing but a diversion strategy to mask my inability to be still and feel safe. This is totally wicked but real.

So much of my identity, I am finding, was associated with work. It was, in fact, more than associated; it was ingrained in my job. Like under the skin. Not having a title and a business card are huge. Suffering from this withdrawal is not necessarily healthy; nor is it easy to admit; but nevertheless, it is true.

To some people, not having an agenda driven by the business or anything to deliver on a deadline is equally difficult. I can deal with that part fairly well. I can create my own agenda, no problem. However, not being associated with a job is odd, uncomfortable. It can be liberating, filled with possibilities, and yes, a nice break. But, it is also destabilizing.

Think of it as a reversed Caribbean vacation. Normally, stress decreases with every day spent on the beach. In this case, stress increases with the return-to-work date approaching because you have no idea what you are going back to, or even, when you will return.

It takes some getting used to.

For now, I pack my swim gear and head out to the pool. I am on sabbatical after all.

It is early in the afternoon. So many people are on the sea wall that changing lanes is a risky business; bicycles are all over the place. As I get to English Bay, I flash back to my very first visit to Vancouver over fifteen years ago, and how I instantly fell in love with the city. It was a similarly gorgeous September day, middle of the week, and I was meeting a friend on the beach. I remember asking whether that day was a day off.

"Why?" he asked.

"Because, there seems to be more people on bikes and on the beach than at work . . . ."

There was this unmistakable sense of a weekend in the air. Today feels just the same, and now I have grown accustomed to it, but it still works its magic on me. I am reminded of the reasons why I moved here. It is the West Coast.

Now, finally, I have time to enjoy it.

I make it to the Vancouver Aquatic Centre. As I enter the building, the smell of chlorine sets my mood instantly. This is good!

Swimming is like rollerblading or cross-country skiing: after a while, the endorphins kick in and you forget that you are in your body. Your mind roams freely. Being able even for a mere hour to let your mind escape on a regular basis is beyond beneficial. My theory is that it stretches your life, potentially saves your marriage, and delays any major blow out at work. It is that good.

Amazing—all that your mind can think of and is willing to contemplate when it is detached from the necessity of having to be real. Endorphins will do that. Times like these I truly believe I could be a prima ballerina, a main character in the latest Broadway show, or face a standing ovation at Carnegie Hall.

It is free thinking at its best.

I get home to find out that the technician is coming tonight to set up my home PC, laptop, and BlackBerry, and not tomorrow as initially planned.

Now, computer techs are like teenagers wanting to talk. When they are ready, you never let that opportunity pass. You drop everything else and accommodate their schedules.

I am willing to do that; however, I am less thrilled with the news that I need to get a piece of software before he can set up my computer.

I am training myself not to expect the worst in everything these days. I am not sure why doing so is a second nature of mine, but it is. When it comes to technology, I clearly expect hardships. So, when the technician says I am missing one piece of hardware, I immediately go into this "I knew it" mood, and write off the rest of the day as being one big pile of frustrations.

Shame on me!

I want to put my best foot forward. I call the store to make sure it has the part in stock. The technical sales representative actually remembers me from yesterday, and get this, tells me he will wait for me before ending his shift. Imagine that!

I quickly change and hop on the bus, where I bump into Joel, Julie's friend from college.

Joel stayed at our place two semesters in a row last year because he had just moved into the city from up north for the beginning of the school year. Finding a place to live in Vancouver that will allow you to save enough money to afford such luxuries as food and heat is a difficult endeavor. It takes time.

So, the deal was every time I was away (and I was gone a lot), my daughter would upgrade to my bedroom, and he would take hers. Yes. I know. But this is truly how it went. Shame on you for thinking otherwise!

My only requirement was that they made sure every time I came home, no one was in my bed, and the sheets were clean. Kind of a twisted Goldilocks deal! Worked out fine for everyone. I am mentioning this because I realize, as I walk away from him and into the store, how nice it felt to be able to help, and how much more traffic was in my life when I had a job and kids at home.

Anyway, I am in and out of the store in no time. They were expecting me, and installed everything in a flash. I am thrilled to find out that people care. Were they like that before and I did not notice? Has my attitude anything to do with it? Does expecting good stuff increase the likelihood of getting some?

Conversely, does walking into a store with a "Don't you dare feed me bullshit" look on your face enhance the possibilities of getting some?

It is highly unlikely that they would have all turned nice since I started my sabbatical. Was I too engrossed in my own issues and racing life to notice? What if people are likeable or obnoxious depending on how I see or approach them, and the way I see them depends on how I feel? Does this possibility make a good case for healthy living?

I am thinking it does.

Heading home. I have not had dinner yet, and the technician should be there any minute now. Take out to the rescue again. What can I say?

It is late when he leaves. I am tired but very pleased. It was a pleasant evening. I learned a lot. We exchanged on multiple topics. What impressed me most, other than his knowledge and the quality of his work, was his kindness.

Another caring person? My goodness, they all seem to be coming out of the woodwork.

Thursday, September 23

I keep cramming everything into the same day as if there is no tomorrow. I have clearly not warmed up to the reality that I have time now.

I make my way down to the garage, carrying my swim bag, my office equipment to be dropped at FedEx, my briefcase since I have a scheduled meeting to attend, and my purse. I also have to make it to the shop to exchange my mobile phone. Did I say it is not working?

I can tell this day is perfectly well-positioned to go down the drain in no time fast!

And indeed, it is starting to go that way . . . . First I have a late start and have to skip FedEx. I am not surprised. In fact, I suspect this skip may be intentional, subconscious perhaps, but intentional all the same. It may be an attempt to bypass the incredibly uneasy feeling of wrapping the last three years of my life in a box stamped "custom clear!" and dropping it in a mailbox.

Then I suffer through the meeting with my financial planner. How boring.

Then I make it to the store to exchange my phone, but of course, they cannot fix or exchange it. Only the original point of sale can do that.

Have you ever noticed how easy it is to buy these things, but how particularly challenging to get help once you have paid for them?

I can't make it back to the original store now because I am running late for lunch with a friend. I need that lunch break more than I need to face the sales clerk. The phone will have to wait. However, my friend does not show up. Of course, I cannot call him. I do not have a phone. I end up waiting thirty minutes in the lobby, and then leave. I could go into the bar and wait for him there, but my thoughts are, given the frame of mind I am in, that if I go in, there is no telling when I am coming out. Better to skip that and go home.

Now that I have recovered some time, I gather all the self-control I can muster and decide to stop at the store on my way home to exchange my mobile phone. I promise myself to behave and not to make a scene. I will be patient.

The salesperson looks at me suspiciously, tries to convince me that I did something to the phone, but finally, thirty minutes later, I am sent home with a new one. Success!

I must admit, though, I barely made it without running the risk of getting my picture in the paper the next morning. I had to remind myself that patience is a virtue and that people are well-intentioned. When I fall out of patience or understanding, it is because of my own shortcomings. Not theirs. I don't always believe this but it helps to try!

Friday September 24

Since I never made it to the pool yesterday, I am still trying to make it today. My ex used to say that I could be so stubborn at times . . . there might be some truth to that after all!

As I finish my morning coffee, I get busy setting up my new phone with all my personal settings. BlackBerry has a neat feature called the password keeper. I painstakingly enter all my passwords in as they are the most important data I have. Once I am done, I test my phone. The thing will not ring, and when trying to sync it with my computer, it crashes. A hot flash comes over me. Who painted my walls red? Can a mobile phone thrown forcefully from ten feet away break a plate glass window?

Evidently, I am not ready to be facing frustrations. I have not been long enough on sabbatical yet to deal with this kind of frustration. I want someone else to take care of it. I want a speed dial on my phone with a friendly voice at the other end saying, "How can I help?"

I try to call the service provider for assistance, but it is an automated service (Oh, joy!). I oblige. For starters, it insists on not recognizing my ten-digit phone number. I am pretty sure it won't help if I make one up.

Then I go online in an attempt to bypass that issue, but I run into the same problem. It will not recognize my number either. Then I find the nearest store and call to see whether anyone would recognize a human being if I showed up at the counter? They assure me they can help. "Come on over," they say.

At last, a break!

Amazing how dealing with humans has become a last resort.

That store is halfway between my place and the pool. Perfect. I pack my swim gear, take my phone, and off I go. I will have time to do both before lunch.

"Can't set the ring tone," he says. "There is a problem with the phone," he says.

How predictable!

"You must go back to the original store!" he says. I raise my hand. Enough. I have heard enough. I know the drill. You guys all went to the same school.

I grab the phone and storm out of the store. I miss the IT department, I miss my secretary, and I miss being pulled away into a meeting and being able to delegate this crap to someone else . . . .

But there is only me. Frustrated, irritated me.

Since I have a lunch date at noon, going back to the store again kills my pool session. So, here I am, walking, rather charging, all the way back and up town, with my swim gear in tow, to go get my phone fixed. I am furious.

By the time I get there, I am soaked. Not from the rain, but from my own perspiration. The walk turns out to be quite a work-out! At least I get this much out of it.

So the phone is damaged. "Of course, it is damaged! I could have told you that!" I feel like saying. I have to provide significant proof, again, that this is not the result of my own stupidity. No, I did not drop it in the fish tank, did not download unusual software, or pry it open with a screwdriver. I actually did not even get around to using the damn thing yet, except, of course, for loading all my passwords information. Stop trying to make me feel like an idiot. I don't need help to do that.

After what seems an eternity, the tech announces that, unfortunately, he cannot retrieve any of the information I have uploaded. No, it is not just a matter of exchanging a Sim card. However, he says, in an effort to comfort me, since he believes I have undoubtedly loaded the information on my computer, it can be retrieved from my PC and transferred to the new phone (if you are counting, this will be the third phone.)

This guy is giving me way too much credit. Who said I had the data transferred onto my computer?

He hands the phone back to me with what appears to be an expectation of gratitude. I beg to differ. I am still up a creek without a paddle here. Damn. Damn. Damn.

I find it hugely ironic that we call these things "smart" phones. Normally, smart to me means good, but as it relates to a phone, it just does not evoke the same thing at all! Truly, all I want is for the thing to work. That's it! Pretty straightforward I should think. It does not need to cook breakfast or sing songs!

So, as the story goes, I no longer have any of my passwords information on file.

I refuse to be told that this information is lost. Like a kid crying for grape juice at a restaurant that only has apple or orange juice, I know, from having been there myself, that there comes a time as a parent when you simply have to say, "Suck it up, honey; there ain't any!" And move on.

The tech has actually reached that point with me.

I am so upset. I just want to be left alone. I want my days to be simple. I don't want any such aggravations. I am willing to go with less in my life, but I insist that what I have works . . . . I want my grape juice. I want it on ice with a straw! I want it now!

Enough already!

The store changes my phone again, but now I don't even want to set it up. I am so sick of it all. "Make sure it rings, receives, and sends, and the voicemail is activated." That's all I care about. To hell with the rest. I throw it in my purse and head back home.

I have barely enough time to get back, shower, change, and head out again for my lunch date.

I am meeting a former colleague from Philadelphia who is in town for the weekend. We go to my favorite restaurant in Stanley Park. The walk is beneficial. I feel a lot calmer by the time I get there, and even better once I leave after a long, copious, pleasant lunch.

Oh, the luxury of time!

As I get home, I am suddenly exhausted. I don't know if I'll ever get used to this roller-coaster lifestyle. I am up. I am down. I don't know what is going on. I feel overwhelmed. I am leaving for two weeks shortly, heading east, and I still have a lot to do. Reinventing your life is a busy business. Until you realize that you don't have to do it all in the next few days, it can be daunting.

It is really hard to admit that such petty little things as a malfunctioning phone drag me down. That, more than the work to be done, weighs on my spirit. What used to be trivial before has shifted to a main source of activities, it seems. I have this uncontrollable fear that my life will become small and insignificant, and therefore, I frantically work at immediately overcoming any such hurdles for fear they will stay and become my new reality. The shift from the busy, buzzing, everybody wanting a piece of me every day to being on my own, by myself, with no one, other than my loved ones, needing anything from me, is a scary place to be. It is a huge adjustment. I am like your typical neurotic salesman who becomes hyperactive every time someone so much as looks at him. He becomes loud and in your face.

I feel that way. I am craving attention.

I need to learn to deal with this change, but I don't know how to do it. What if I did nothing? What if I just let it all be and waited to see how it sorts itself out? What difference would it make if I just put the phone down, stayed a few more days without a working phone, and waited for the solution to come along? Would it work?

Somehow, it sounds tempting. My best strategy at this stage is to lie down and take a nap. The heck with this; I am on sabbatical.

Friday October 1

I board my usual 11 a.m. flight to Montreal. It is still difficult not to reach for my laptop and catch up on my email. To sit still for five hours and simply read, watch a movie, or even more challenging, simply listen to music, does not come naturally. This is a discovery for me. I need to be busy even when I am not. What's with that?

There is that incredible sense of "must do; must take advantage of that idle time" syndrome. I am actually surprised. I thought I was always that calm, easygoing person. I find I can be quite wired. Unwiring me is not as easy as I thought it would be.

The irony is that while I was in that fast mode, wanting to catch up and stay on top of things (mostly at work), I did not ever, ever catch up unless I played alone while nobody else was. The only time to get ahead was the weekend or the middle of the night. Then, of course, I might have won the catch-up game that day, but lost on other fronts such as sleep, relationships, and health just to name a few.

Turns out everybody only has so many marbles. You can put them all on the work game and have none left for other things . . . or you can spread them differently. The art is to know how to spread them and avoid spreading them too thin on anything.

In my last job, I had the benefit of working with an executive coach. Although I always appreciated the time spent with her, one thing that positively drove me crazy was how she repeatedly told me, "You can do anything you want, remember? It's your choice." I actually never believed her. I did not think it was true.

Now, at long last, I am starting to understand what she meant. In the end, you choose where you are and what you do. You do. If you stop long enough and look really hard into what keeps you where you are, you will find that it is you.

An ugly thought when you happen to hate where you are!

So, if you don't like what you do, you change. If you don't like where you are, you move. Sounds simple. Of course, a myriad of logistical issues surround making a change, but bottom line: she was right.

This is your call.

Sunday October 3

I am now in Montreal. It is cold and wet. I spend most of the afternoon with Tem, shopping for furniture, beddings, pots and pans and assorted household goods. I hate shopping. Did I say this already?

Only Tem can make shopping remotely enjoyable. Three hours later, I have everything I need, arranged for delivery, and have totally alienated my credit card. It is a good day.

I have a condo in Montreal which I use when I visit my family and friends. Since I frequently travel to the southeastern United States on business, I sometimes head north to be in Montreal before making my way back home to the West Coast—thus the condo (and the frequent flyer status!).

Now, I no longer work and no longer use the condo since I stay at Tem's place when I am in town. Common sense is to sell or at least rent it, furnished preferably; thus, the shopping. It was missing a few items.

You would think that shopping for furniture and household goods could be associated with a day off, or a good time, but to me, honestly, it still feels like work.

Actually, I am starting to wonder what will have to happen for me to feel like I am not working.

How do I define work to start with anyway? A chore I need to get done so I can move on to the things I really like? That does not seem right. A gathering of endless frustrations that get in the way of doing what I truly want to do? That is no better and certainly not healthy. How is it with the people who say their jobs do not even feel like work? What do they know that I don't? How much "undoing" will I have to do before I get to the real thing? When was the last time I loved my job so much it did not feel like work?

I want that feeling again.

Tonight, I am meeting with a former colleague and a long-time friend for dinner. She and I used to work together many years ago. I was her client and we became friends. Part of my makeover, as I call it, and the next thing on my radar, after resting my body and re-claiming my new space as a result of being an empty nester, is to reconnect with friends I have not been keeping in touch with over the last few years. I also want to expand my network. I don't want to grow old as one of two people. Every time I meet someone, I try to envision myself in his or her job or life. I ask all kinds of questions. Would I like it? Do I have what it takes? Would I be able to do it? How does this person make it work? I figure once I have been around enough people, I will have a pretty comprehensive kaleidoscope of jobs and life scenarios. From that collection, I should be able to put one together for myself.

This is the extent of my plan at the moment.

So I am meeting with her because it is her birthday and I happen to be in Montreal, because I enjoy her company, and also to scout around and see whether there may be some synergy between her and me, work-wise. She has quite an appetite for life. She is full of projects, and her energy and passion are contagious. She is a feel-good kind of person. She runs her own business and has done so for years. She has a son in China, business partners all over the world, and a romance going on in Casablanca.

My kind of girl!

The more we speak, the more I realize that her business would be the perfect platform for me to launch a group coaching business. My memory takes me back in a flash to a conversation I had some time ago with the executive forum's leader. Wow! Could this be an opportunity for me to start something like a coaching business? So soon? I quickly find myself trying to make it work as if I had to take everything that comes my way. I feel uneasy. Isn't this a bit early into the sabbatical to be committing to moving and all? Did I weigh all my options yet?

Hardly.

She quickly picks up on my warning bells going off. She offers me an out by agreeing that we should revisit this topic in the New Year after I have had a few months off. Yeah! Let's wait until the New Year. That way I can continue to procrastinate.

Sometimes, admitting your fears buys you time to deal with them!

In fact, I am confirming the theory that in order to be able to move forward successfully, one needs to let go of the past. Nothing new here. An obvious statement if ever there were one, but believe me, reading it and living it are two different realities!

My desire to procrastinate and sit on this coaching idea stems from my being unsure that I want to let go of all that needs to go in order for me to make the shift from a jet-set corporate life to a self-employed "do it all yourself and good luck with that" model! I sense something terribly final is in this decision . . . and final is scary. Every time. Besides, self-employment does not come with a 911 number. You're on your own, baby, when you make that jump! You just hope your parachute will open. So making the decision to jump can, in fact, be paralyzing.

When I see myself stuck that way, not wanting to move forward, but unable to go back, I am reminded of my friend Michel, who at the time was more than a friend.

He was trying to help me move beyond my fears. We were hiking in the woods, as we often liked to do, no rush, no pressure, talking about fears I had that I seemed unable to face. We were walking along the river and came across a bridge. He stopped. "Wait here," he said and went into the woods to grab a stick. He came back and handed it to me.

I gave him a puzzled look. "Throw it in the river," he said. So I did. Then we stood there.

"Now what?" I asked.

"Now we stay here until it comes back," he replied.

"The stick?"

He nodded.

"Well, that is stupid," I said.

He smiled. "Life is no different, honey. Gone is gone. Time to move on."

Why is everybody else so smart about my life?

At this point though, it is not that simple to me. I need more time. I do not know what is right for me, nor what should I do. It drives me crazy not to know. Problem-solving was always my forte. Whatever happened to that?

Tuesday October 5

Today, I borrow Tem's car. I am determined to conclude the household goods shopping spree for the condo. Not least on the list are the TV set and DVD player. For that part, I have scheduled thirty minutes—about all I can take of multiple screens and loud soundtrack in a department store.

So I head out to the nearest electronics store. My view is that a TV is a TV is a TV. I think I find what I want. All I need now is a sales rep to sell it to me, and if it is not asking for too much, perhaps answer a few questions.

I can't find anyone to help. That is a rather common situation for a buyer. I know that, but today, I don't deal with it so well.

I find a clerk:

"Can someone help me in the electronics department, please?"

"No," he simply replies.

I can tell. This already has the right ingredients to turn into a bad scenario. Luckily, I know how to play nice.

"I am terribly sorry to bother you, but if possible, I would like to spend upwards of a thousand dollars here today, and I need someone to help me do it. Do you think it would be possible to get some assistance?"

"No. The guy did not come in today," he says.

Now I miss Tem, or someone to whisper in my ear, to remind me that it is in my best interest to stay cool and stay put. Where are my friends when I need them?

"Perhaps someone else could come in and help," I insist.

Abruptly, he picks up the phone and asks for assistance in the electronics department. Now we are making progress.

Fifteen minutes go by. I am still standing here. My ex was right. I can be stubborn. At last, a lady comes in and offers her help.

"Are you knowledgeable in electronics?" I ask since I have a few questions to ask.

"No. I work in the shoe department," she answers.

!!!

Now, under any other circumstances, I would always welcome someone with an appreciation for shoes, but at this very moment, not so much!

Long story short, I buy the TV set and DVD player from the shoe lady. I am embarrassed to say that other than the size and price, I know remarkably little about what they can do. I don't care. I don't watch TV. Someone else will, and based on the price I paid, it darn well better work.

However, today again, my day feels more like a grocery list I have to go through, and my only satisfaction is the ability to cross items off it. It is no fun and breeds a sense of guilt. I can't help thinking that a lot of people would much rather be shopping on a Tuesday afternoon, knowing they would be free after lunch, than be at work. So, why am I not enjoying this? Why don't I feel like a million bucks for being where everybody else wants to be? Why do I even care?

Thursday October 7

Today is autumn at its best. I drove to Quebec City yesterday, my hometown. Before heading out for the restaurant where I am having lunch with a former supplier who also ended up being a friend, I go for a long walk. I miss this time of year in the East now that I live on the West Coast. The air is crisp and fragrant. The sound of leaves crumbling, as I drag my feet through heaps of them, takes me years back into my childhood. If I close my eyes, I can smell the leaves burning.

I meet my friend. We connect just like before. In no time, we are talking shop, potential business, mutual colleagues, and I find myself excited and happy. I feel energized. How quickly I latch on to anything that looks like work is beginning to worry me. I seem to forget how far Quebec City is from Vancouver. Again, I do not screen this conversation against my what-do-I-want-to-do-when-I-grow-up lenses. Don't I have any discrimination?

I find it hard sometimes to differentiate between the reasons why I do not want to go back to work for fear of finding myself in a less than desirable environment, and the need to take a break and regroup, also known as a legitimate break, before heading out again. At times, the two become confused. How will I know when sufficient rest and reflection have taken place and it is time to move on? Does one know when one is truly ready? Is this like asking your mother how you will know when the boyfriend you are dating is your husband-to-be?

As we get ready to leave, I automatically reach out for my business card. Gasp! No business card.

How did I not think of getting some made? But what would I write beside my name? My home address? My favorite color? I mean, I could write anything! My fields of expertise maybe . . . but I have not decided yet what I want to focus on . . . and I don't want just a plain card. I want a nice card. An interesting one. I will need to think of a design that would represent me, my business. But, what business? For now, my phone number on a napkin will have to do.

Friday October 8

I am heading back to Montreal for the weekend. I drive casually along. There is no hurry. This pace does feel good. I find myself thinking of my former job and missing some of it.

Who would have thought?

Mostly, I miss the colleagues and the environment outside of work, such as a few favorite restaurants, the walks on the beach since I was so often in Florida, the easy shopping (shoes, you know, and a favorable currency exchange), the hotel staff greeting me at the door; we had almost become family after all these visits. I guess what I miss is the comfort of a routine; going back to familiar places, going through a drill where there are more known than unknown quantities. Unknown gets to you after a while. Comfort exists in going through thoughtless motions, and comfort breeds security.

Once work stops, you immediately become master of your time; a constant fantasy for most full-time workers. In my case, that dream became a reality, and it is now challenging me. Time, like anything else, needs to be managed to be efficient. Not even time flows freely.

Bummer!

Of course, you can plan to be on vacation, and then it is okay not to manage it. But, vacations have a start and an end date. A sabbatical, at least mine, only has a start date . . . no end date yet. Some like it that way; others don't. For me, this time is similar to those contests where you have a few minutes to run up and down the aisles and fill your cart as much as possible. Whatever you are able to put in when the bell rings is yours to keep.

This sabbatical feels the same to me. This is a once-in-a-lifetime break, and if I don't take full advantage of it while I can, the bell will ring, and only a few things will be in my basket.

At least, that is my fear.

So I am going at it the way a snow plow faces a snow bank: head on!

I think about all I ever wanted to do when I was still at work and dreaming I wouldn't be. That trip to Europe, that kitchen renovation, that gym program, the new bike, all these new restaurants, and now I have time to sit and look around and see and discover all that I did not know was out there before and now want a piece of. It takes planning and restraint, believe me. Two items I am typically low on.

Saturday October 9

Still in Montreal. My sister flew in last night. I pick her up this morning. We are going to surprise Mom and Dad by showing up in our PJs for breakfast! Just for the hell of it.

She and I have always lived away from home. The highlights of our trips back home have often been to find ourselves in the morning, at the breakfast table with Mom. We would talk and laugh for hours. Now our parents have moved out of their house and live in a retirement home. We can no longer stay with them. There is no spare room (thus my condo). We all miss the cozy breakfasts.

So, this morning, we come into the building dressed in gym gear. We walk past the reception and take the elevator one floor short of my parents' apartment. Then we take the stairwell up to their floor, so we can change away from the hallway crowd. So the scene is as follows: two grown women with pants down to their ankles and sweaters over their heads, trading their running shoes for polar slippers and laughing so hard they need to lean against the wall not to fall.

We sneak out of the stairwell, run to the apartment door, and ring the doorbell. When Mom opens it, we are both standing there in our PJs, claiming our breakfast!

We feel like kids again, minus the sibling rivalry!

We have such a pleasant morning. It is so much fun to have fun! Fun is one of the first things that typically gets kicked out of your life when you move into the "busy world."

Very refreshing.

Noon. Before I turn into a pumpkin (the daylight version) I kiss everyone goodbye. I must be on my way.

Tem and I are leaving for La Malbaie again. He has a business function there for the next two days, and then we will stretch the stay into the long weekend. It is our Thanksgiving weekend.

We get there just in time to unpack, change, and join his colleagues for cocktails.

Now, here is a novelty. Yet another one. Something I have not experienced in years. I am here as Tem's spouse. "Good evening; please meet my friend; she is . . . my friend." What else can you say about me? She is my retired friend? My unemployed friend? My empty nester friend? Now, I know this situation is not any different from any spouse attending any social function; however, it has not happened to me in years, and quite frankly, I have not missed being introduced as somebody else's somebody!

The disturbing fact to me is that I have worked quite hard at building my own identity, of which my job was a part. Now that I am no longer employed, I feel as if I may have lost a significant chunk of that identity. Something is wrong with that picture.

Will the remedy be to get another job and transfer that void onto the next job, or is it to recognize that being me suffices for anything I want to do or be in my life? Why do I need a title? Somehow, I feel this thought is leading to a slippery road. What would have to happen, I wonder, for me to like, approve of, and be comfortable with "Meet my friend Gisele" and nothing more? I conveniently say that others expect a description of who you are, but really, is it them or is it me? Evidently, I have more thinking to do here.

Luckily, this group is an exceptionally nice and particularly interesting group, so it is not about them. It is about me looking at them from the angle of someone who is counting her losses. Right or wrong, this is how I feel. Someone who has not yet figured out how to present herself.

This too will pass. Patience is something else I am learning.

Cocktail hour is over. We quickly go up to our rooms and change. We have a black tie dinner to attend.

A pleasant evening it is, and a busy one at that. It is now two in the morning, and Tem and I are winding down, sipping a last nightcap in the hotel lounge. Most everyone else is gone. The evening is now quiet, and the darkness on the other side of the panoramic windows is only broken by flickering lights from the ships on the river.

A peaceful moment.

In comes this man in worn-out jeans, oversized T-shirt, and a baseball cap worn backward. His dog is in tow. He seems to be looking for something. He appears in a hurry and somewhat lost. I am thinking he is a homeless local chap taking advantage of the hotel's warmth and comfort now that most guests are gone.

He walks directly to the grand piano, regrettably standing silent in the corner of the room. Without even sitting down, he reaches for the keyboard and starts playing. What suddenly fills the room is a very beautiful rendition of Liszt's *Liebesträume*, the third solo—the most famous.

He instantly takes this evening to another level.

Abruptly, halfway through the piece, he stops, calls his dog sound asleep under the piano, and walks away.

"You can't stop just like that," I say.

"Sorry; I did not think anyone was here."

He is sorry! He must be kidding.

We invite him to stay and play some more. He sits down and proceeds with pieces from Brahms and Beethoven. The passion and delight flowing from him are tangible.

We offer him a drink the way you drop a five dollar bill in a guitar case on the street. Somehow, we feel we owe him something, and to be totally honest, we also think he may not have had the luxury of a nice drink in a while.

He orders ginger ale!

Turns out, he is a guest at the hotel, and being a car mechanic is his means to earning a living, while music is his passion, piano in particular. He lives with his family north of Montreal; he owns a house and a few pianos. In his spare time, he disassembles and rebuilds them just for the love of it.

Well, this man evidently has no identity issues, and it all sits comfortably with him.

A lesson to be learned: Doesn't matter whom you appear to be; it is who you are and what you have to offer that matters.

We all know that. Sometimes, we just need to be reminded, again and again.

Sunday October 10

Today, Tem and I are deliberately lazy. We let the morning stretch endlessly, at least until noon, when we have lunch with friends in St. Irénée, a quiet town perched on the cliff overlooking the St. Lawrence. We need to get ready.

These friends, next to my family, are the pillars of my life. I have known them for over forty years. I cannot imagine my life without them, and yet I have lived most of it away from them.

Whenever I see them, I think it is time for me to come home. Today is no exception. Time with them is good for my soul.

Right after lunch, we head back to Montreal. I have a family dinner tonight. Mom and Dad, my two brothers, my sister, and me.

Being away from my parents in their old age is a continuous concern of mine. I am lucky that, despite their age, they are not old yet. But, it will come. So, when I think of my professional life going forward, location is a big item. It concerns my friends. It also concerns my family.

The more time I spend in Vancouver, the more I feel as if home is in that city. Yet, the more I age, the more I am pulled toward Montreal.

Sigh.

Tuesday October 12

Because of the long Thanksgiving weekend, I could not get a flight back to Vancouver today; so nothing is on my agenda until the phone rings at 9 a.m. It is the realtor. She may have an interested tenant for my condo here in Montreal. Good news, except he wants to come in for a visit at eleven this morning, and if interested, he wants to move in on Friday this week.

A moment of panic is closely followed by strong denial. NO! I just want the day off! When you open yourself to all possibilities, you have to expect to be tossed around a little bit. Today is such a day.

As always, reason kicks in. I rush through the condo, clean, pick up, store, file—all in time for the visit.

It is now a done deal. He will move in on Friday.

Somehow, a tenant wanting to move in feels like a tidal wave. Even though the decision to rent is mine, and it is a sound business decision, I am sad to rent. I like this condo. Every time I pick up a rental car at the airport, drive to my place away from home, and show up at the garage door to activate it by remote control, I feel like a queen.

Who wouldn't want to hold on to that? Renting it today feels like giving it away. It feels like a good thing coming to an end. Another one. Maybe it is just another loss I have to deal with and adjust to.

Interesting how these losses (the condo, my job) are actually losses I have chosen and welcomed, and if I had to do them over again, I would do the same. Moreover, both cases lead to upsides as well, but initially, they feel like a loss. There is no getting around this feeling.

By 7 p.m. when Tem comes to pick me up, the place is sanitized, all personal and precious items packed and stored, bedding changed, suitcases packed, windows washed, contract signed . . . condo rented.

I am sad. Go figure!

Well, actually, I don't need time to figure it out. It is pretty obvious what is going through my head, except I don't really want to be listening to it. That's all. If I listen to it, then it will be more difficult to ignore it. Sometimes a whole lot of comfort can be found in sticking your head in the sand. Trust me.

Truthfully, there is a lot more to this condo than just its proximity to my mom and dad and that it allows me to visit my friends and children. It is also my back-up plan for retirement. I bought it thinking that when or if my retirement money runs out one of these days—since I don't have all that much money, and I expect to live to a ripe old age, if nothing has changed in my life, meaning, I am still the sole provider to my existence—then I can always sell my condo in Vancouver and move here and live until I break the Guinness world record for old age, and I'll be fine. You see, not having the rug pulled out from under my feet ever again, where I would have to scramble to reinvent my life, again, is a goal. It is okay for me to do so in my forties and fifties when I am ready and able to do it. It would be another thing when I am old and unwilling to face the unknown.

But now, and here comes the punch line, I have Tem in my life. We are serious about growing old together. I know we are, but somehow I don't seem truly to grasp it. Something in me continues to struggle with the prospect of a good life. How dangerous it would be to truly believe it. That is what is behind the discomfort around renting my condo. Now I will have to believe in the good life, and that does not come easy for me.

A bit sick. It is.

However, my mind is made up. I am doing this. In this year of transition, I am the witness of an increased battle between my head and my heart. Before, I would always let my head win. After all, I had kids to feed and a mortgage to pay. Now, I can truly give full control to my heart, and yet, sometimes I still don't think I can trust it. I'm not always very grown up I find!

Monday October 18

I am back in Vancouver, and as always, I take in the city, its beauty, the enjoyment of being by the water. It rocks my soul.

Feeling relaxed, comfortable, and master of my own time all have a really nice ring to them. However, where the tune goes a little bit out of key is when I try to reconcile what I do with a purpose. You know; the need to be needed. Where is all of this leading me?

I wonder though. Do I honestly need to know the answer to that question?

This is a recurring theme, I know, and I am only now beginning to pay attention to it. More often than I care to admit, not knowing the purpose of what I do, or where it is leading, influences my ability to enjoy it. Maybe that is normal. Is it?

Here is something even more twisted. When I was employed, it was easy to enjoy a day off, except that I seldom had one. Now, down time is all I have, and I do everything I can to turn it into work.

Sick again?

Last night, I attended a function at the Museum of Anthropology where I met this most interesting man—Ph.D. in physics, European background, spent most of his working career in the States, recently married, and father of two young children, passionate about a myriad of things, not the least of which include the environment and education. We thoroughly enjoyed our conversation.

It made me realize how I miss having such lively and challenging encounters. Maybe I should sit on boards, volunteer at some think tanks, go back to school, write a sequel to *War and Peace* . . . . I need to embark on something big! Cruising along has never been my pace. If comfort were a finite line, then my preferred zone would be just short of the edge . . . !

I can't help but notice that I always feel like I should do something different or something more than what I am doing at the moment, and frankly, it does not feel good. It is like never being in the right place. It gets tiring, and I don't think it is healthy at all. Is this everyone's lot, or is it part of my ADD brain?

So the time has come for one more consideration now. Taking a break, embracing my new empty nester status, and connecting with others all came naturally. Connecting with myself and figuring out truly, deeply in my heart of hearts, what I see for my life (they call it vision) and why I would want to do it (purpose) are the goals now, and while I am on the topic of goals, I need to find my big hairy audacious goal (aka BHAG!). That is the one that takes you the furthest. That process does not come naturally. Inevitably, I knew this sabbatical would lead to defining my goals. Everything in life does. I will need to sit down, look myself in the eyes, and figure them out.

Wednesday October 20

I wonder whether everyone struggles with this idea of finding one's passion. It always feels like everybody else has everything squared away. I remember how speechless I was when my fifteen-year-old son told me, after I had been desperately trying to find interests and activities for him and suggested going to the library to pick up some books, "Mom, I don't even know what I like to read." Mind you, the library may not have been the most exciting plan for a teenager, granted, but nevertheless, for someone like me who is a hardcore booklover, I could not understand that response at all. How can you not know what you like? Today my son is a very well-read individual, and his bookshelves are much more impressive than mine. But here I am today. It is my turn to be on the lookout, and my attempts at going back to the pool, the gym, practicing piano, connecting with friends, talking to strangers, discovering new music, leafing through various universities' curriculums, is nothing less than an attempt to find something that will ignite a part of my brain or heart that has probably gone to sleep over the years, or worse, never woken up. It is probably similar to recovering from amnesia. You try to work your way backward into your life, hoping to find the missing pieces, or where you took the wrong turn. It is a marvellously exciting time, I must say, if you are willing to be patient.

Unfortunately, that is not a quality I was born with. But patience is something I am trying to acquire. Working on it.

How did I find myself here? I am not sure. It may be a function of time, pure and simple, or it may be the result of slowly shutting down some parts of my inner self simply because I had no time or there was no space for it. It is all part of the delicate balance of knowing who I am and being able to be me. It probably results from the choices I made, and the people I associate with, by choice or by obligation. They have a front row seat in my life, and they can be instrumental in helping or deterring me. In the end though, it is my stuff. No one else can be me, but me. At least I've got this squared away.

I look up. It is nearly four o'clock. Disbelief. I have been at my computer since very early this morning, working on a new project: writing, maybe a blog, maybe a book, maybe nothing, but writing it is. I am totally consumed by it. I have a headache, mostly due to starvation, and my vision is blurred from all these hours looking at the screen. Moreover, today is a beautiful day, the kind of day that compels me to go out and play. I should be outside. I literally force myself out of the house. I feel guilty when I don't go out on a sunny day. I have the good fortune of living in an extraordinary neighborhood. Beauty is everywhere you look, from tree-covered streets and heritage buildings to luxuriously healthy plants and majestic mountain views. Even if you don't like going for walks or a run, here you do. Despite all this, I mostly wander around until I am able to allow myself back in. There is no energy for me anywhere else than at my computer. I want to write. That is all I want to do.

Writing!

Here is something that does not feel like work. It feels like I had to dig for a long time to find it, particularly when I did not actually know what I was digging for.

Who cares how you find what you are looking for so long as you find it? There is no patent on searching!

Friday, October 22

I am still high on writing. You may think this sudden interest is coming out of nowhere, but honestly, all my life, I have been writing—in my head, that is! I thought of stories when I sat in airport lounges, waiting to board planes, when we taxied and took off and no computers were allowed, and therefore, I could not work; I thought of writing when sitting in the cab on my way to wherever, at the dentist, while rollerblading, when swimming laps, while rocking my babies to sleep . . . .

However, writing is something I always did late at night before turning in, or when overwhelmed with whatever—I can always think of something to overwhelm me—and have to bring down the pressure gauge.

Whatever I wrote about, I never associated it with a normal daily activity. Now I can.

I think this discovery may be a first hint; a first real piece of the puzzle to define what I need to integrate into my business, and into my day-to-day life. Because of what it means to me, and because of the energy and pleasure associated with it, I think I am on to something.

Being the driven individual I am, I can tell it will require some practice. I tend to be bulimic with things I enjoy. It's a balancing act I have never mastered. It will be challenging, no doubt.

It is getting late in the day. I am joining my friends for dinner. There are four of us, at one time all connected through the same job. The group is now expanding thanks to significant others joining in. At times, though, I miss just being the four of us, like in the "good old days."

When I think of maybe leaving Vancouver to establish myself in Montreal, I think of them. They would show up in the loss column.

The more I toy with this dilemma of where I should live, the more I am convinced that I don't want to decide.

Instead, I need to find a professional arena that will allow me to work in both cities. That way, I can cover the expenses of traveling back and forth, and I can grow roots to ensure I never leave either place.

Maybe I will spread myself thinner in the process, but I am ready to give it a try. Besides, thinner has a nice ring to it. Like having your cake and eating it too.

Can't blame me for trying!

Monday October 25

I love to organize my life and take care of the nuisances so they can take care of themselves thereafter . . . . no unpaid bills, no unopened mail, no pending files, etc. In some areas of my life, I don't like surprises.

So, to that end, I am meeting with the financial planner today. Again. I'm not sure this meeting is a good idea. I know what he is going to say, and I don't want to hear it. Besides, the meeting is in the middle of the day and ruins my ability to attend my preferred yoga class, or even to make it to the pool before the late crowd (after-school kids) all come jumping in.

Of course, he is talking to me about taking my severance money and locking it away for years on end, in tax-deferred channels, where the real benefit of such actions will be midway in my retirement, or on my deathbed.

Seriously!

The true, raw, emotional side of me wants to keep that money in the bank, or better yet, in my nightstand drawer, so I can look at it from time-to-time, and keep it there until it runs out, and meanwhile, enjoy a life of writing, yoga, and outdoors living.

My bet is he will not be impressed with my plan!

Now, of course, this plan quickly gets kicked in the ribs by my reason and logic—my two humdrum twins. You won't find more efficient party poopers than them. In all fairness, though, they have served me well in my life so far. Kind of like the friends you hate to love!

Despite the planner being knowledgeable, reasonable, diplomatic, and tactful, I still want to punch him in the teeth. He is making me use my reasonable and rational mind at a time when I am trying really hard to see what life would be like without the humdrum twins for a while, or at least with them in the backseat, instead of the driver's seat.

He is sort of sabotaging my efforts. That is what it feels like. Evidently, trying to be outside the realm of logic and rationality with your financial planner may not be the smartest plan . . . . It might be easier with the interior designer or the seamstress. In any case, he is making me face my ambiguity at a time when I don't want to. Right now, I am in full denial of pretty much anything that has to do with being reasonable; I may as well admit it.

Tuesday October 26

I could not find a *Globe & Mail* yesterday, so I have no paper to read this morning. I know, I know; I can get it online, but I spend enough time as it is in front of that screen . . . a non-virtual morning paper is a luxury I am holding on to. Because I don't have home delivery since I am gone too often, and because I don't get dressed to get out of the house before I have my morning coffee, unless I absolutely have to, I never read today's paper. Yesterday's news is my kind of news.

So, instead, I am catching up with all that accumulated reading material I pile up on my coffee table. Articles from various professionals, experts, gurus, etc.

The more I read, the gloomier it gets as I contemplate a potential career in consulting. Tons of offerings are out there. Consultants of every walk, every area, every specific application. All seem to have a Ph.D. and to have been at it for at least the last twenty-five years. Suddenly, the thought of having to enter that arena feels like fighting my way through a jam-packed, overcrowded entrance to the world's largest football field, just minutes before kick-off . . . . That or 6 a.m. on Black Friday at Macy's. Either one, not good.

It all seems way too hard and next to impossible. What am I thinking? Just because I have been at it all these years as well, minus the Ph.D., will clients select me over the next guy? And how the heck do I know whom my client is?

Remember Waldo? The graphic novel character who was hiding in the background? The aim of the game was to find him. At least he wore a red-striped shirt and a tuque, so if you were patient enough when reading those *Where's Waldo?* books, you could eventually spot him.

Who knows what my clients wear to work?

Maybe I am too old to enter that game? Or am I just too tired this morning?

It all looks somewhat unreachable and nearly impossible. Like looking through a heavy curtain or a thick screen. You can make out the view on the other side, but it sure isn't clear. Will tomorrow draw a clearer picture?

Seriously, I need to engage in something easy and mindless. This is too much thinking.

Email is always a perfect fallback position. I have a new message. A well-known recruiting firm from Montreal is asking me to call back. Turns out it wants me to consider a very nice job in a very nice company. Canada's top fifty. The job is in Montreal; my CV will need to be translated into French. The job starts next month, and I need to be in Montreal next week . . . .

Gasping for air.

Didn't I say I did not want to go back to the corporate world? Did I actually say it, or did I just think it? Was that decided? I need to ask my brain . . . . I try to avoid these decisions myself . . . . Did I say I was ready to move back to Montreal, or is that also under review by the brain board?

I commit to sending my resume because I just can't say no to that kind of a call. I say, however, that I am not available until January; somewhat like coitus interruptus . . . not good! You want to, but you don't. There is no conviction on my part; it almost feels like a duty. The issue is that you think jobs like these may not come your way again for quite a while. Because a lot of people would do back-flips on high heels for that job, I feel I need to be at least considerate. In the end, though, I elect out. I am not ready. I am not excited about it, and should I be told I have the job, I think I would break down and cry . . . So maybe this is a hint!

If I could decide, once and for all in my head, whether or not I will go back to the corporate world, and whether I will live in Vancouver or Montreal, then I think I could enjoy my down time. Until this decision is made, it is hard for me to rest. I hear myself saying this and I recall how people would say that until they had paid off their student loan, their car, and their mortgage, and had at least one promotion, and one more vacation, they would not be ready for a kid, and I would say, "Dream on! You are simply adding up excuses as you get closer to the deadline. I'm not sure I am any different now. Whenever I go into the "when, then," I know I am procrastinating. The fact is I am in a once-in-a-lifetime situation where I am on sabbatical and there is no hurry for me to pull out of it, but I feel like I need to spoil it by worrying about everything. So, as part of my resolution not to think about work and be on sabbatical, I commit to attending the onboarding session from the outplacement service my former employer included in my package. I know there are many who think that the best way to take a break is to turn off the computer and the BlackBerry, send an out of office message, and take off. So attending such classes does not really serve me well. I agree there is a lot of wisdom to that. However, turning everything off only makes sense if you are able to leave the hamster behind . . . .

This hamster is a form of parasite residing permanently in my head, right next to the on/off switch. I suspect some mischievous wandering-by fairy gave it the keys to the control room at the time of my birth.

The hamster and I mostly get along. For the most part, we have learned to live together. Where we run into problems is when I have considerations it does not, such as a body to feed, and rest, a life to lead, and a social life to participate in. All it wants is to work on projects. As much as I would like to, I can't indulge it. So, I am constantly catering to its neurotic behavior.

At this point, my strategy is to feed it so much stuff that it will choke and slow down, and then I'll sneak out while it is digesting . . . . Registering for the transition class at this point will give me a view of what is available and what I will want to participate in. I can always resume in a few months when I am ready to do so. Visibility and projection are what I am after here.

A world of information is in that program, but there are also mandatory actions for me to take, and deadlines to comply with. So, it is more than just fact-gathering; it will require some participation.

That's okay. I am ready for it.

Friday October 29

Church bells are to Montreal what seagulls are to Vancouver. When I sit on the balcony on a Sunday morning, sipping coffee and reading my newspaper and the church bells start ringing, I am five years old all over again. I am wearing my best Sunday shoes, my hair is pulled back in a ponytail, and I am walking to church with my family, most likely trying to beat my sister to the front door!

When I am in Vancouver and wake up to the sound of seagulls, I am an adult who feels good about the life she has chosen!

Although I am trying to avoid making big decisions, one I did make was to maintain my frequent flyer status. If my plans work out, and I get to travel coast-to-coast next year as part of my consulting gig, I will greatly appreciate that status. So, more often than not, I am in Montreal on weekends.

Nice thing about it is that my internal hamster gets bored there, and quite significantly, it slows down. Nobody to pay attention to it, I guess. Hamsters don't know how to deal with the good life either! No deadlines, no rush, not even anything to plan . . . . only *la dolce vita*.

Not having deadlines when I meet with groups of executives in networking events or otherwise often makes me feel uncomfortable. Everyone seems to be struggling with traveling up and down the corporate ladder, and my biggest issue is to learn to be on vacation. My situation feels so self-centered and insignificant compared to everyone else's reality. That difference is a bit of a sting, I must admit. A big sting actually. I feel small among them.

You know, it takes courage to feel small among tall people and still stand up!

Then it takes even more courage to look into what it is that makes me feel small, and makes them look tall in my eyes! This image is getting sticky. Sticky, but quite frankly, downright healthy because if I can hold that thought long enough, I will get to the end of it, and I have a sickening feeling that I know who is at the end of it. Me. Only me.

This thought is mine and mine alone. No one else thinks I am smaller than he or she.

So, if the thought of smallness is mine alone, then all I should have to do is change it! Just think I'm big! No one will ever know the difference!

I am still reflecting on this when my friend from Montreal calls. She is in litigation over a contract particularly significant to her business. She just fired the foreman managing the construction of her house. Her mother-in-law fell, broke her hip, and needs to be admitted to the hospital. Her daughter moved back in with her boyfriend, in my friend's house that is, and she needs to prepare for a presentation to a new client next week. Can I help?

She is a friend. How can I say no? "Send me your stuff."

Monday, November 1

I am expected at the outplacement office for a photo shoot. It offers a complimentary headshot for your business cards, LinkedIn etc. Might as well.

Just as I am leaving, Ed calls. He is coming downtown for a meeting today. Our respective meetings are within a few blocks of each other and at the same time. Perfect!

How is it that you look at yourself every day in the mirror, and therefore, one would assume you are very familiar with your face, but you can't recognize it on a picture? No way! This face can't be mine. It is stiff, tired-looking, and worse, void of any "life." It is one-dimensional! It needs to improve. That too.

Good God! Does one have to improve everything? Can't a few things stay the way they are and be okay? Well, this change will have to come naturally or in my sleep. I am betting that the inside will take care of the outside, or else I haven't got a clue what it will take.

Meanwhile Ed and I meet at this nice Italian café downtown and have cappuccino and biscotti. There is something unmistakably efficient about an Italian environment that makes a woman feel good again. What a nice way to end the morning!

I walk back home. I don't mind the rain. It is refreshing at times. Because I want to make it to the pool before all the swim classes start, and because I don't have any lunch ready at home (I am not talking about this anymore), I stop to buy lunch on the way. Yes. Take out.

As I often do, I surf the web while eating. One of the options I have been toying with is going back to school. Why not? Everything is up for grabs, so I may as well consider that too.

I love learning. Were I independently wealthy, I would be a lifelong student. Among the various programs I am considering, one I am more interested in than others is executive coaching.

I think that choice would make sense to me. Looking back on my career, I can tell that the most lasting element I have found in the corporate world is the individual within. That is also where the biggest leverage is. Not the strategy, not the business plan, not the career path, and not the client's loyalty. All of that dies and is reinvented in two-year cycles it seems—maybe even shorter—pretty much tying in with the CEO's cycle. Where it is certainly worthwhile to invest time, and effort, is in the individual's development.

I want my work to make a lasting difference.

So, coaching is something I like, and believe in. There is a program I have been contemplating for a few years, but never had time for. Today, I realize it starts in two months, and registrations must be completed within twenty-one days.

The alarm bell goes off. Three weeks from now. Ready or not, I need to decide now. At long last! An impulsive decision. Yeah!

I get on the phone. Call my college and university for transcripts, chase former employers down for reference letters, and check with the university to make sure some vacancies still remain for the January program.

"There are," they say. "You must hurry and go online, complete the registration form, make sure to send in your check and all required documents, including your detailed bio, reference letters, transcripts, reasons for applying," etc.

But I also just wanted to be on vacation . . . .

So then why am I doing all of this? Because this program is a one-year program, and even though I have the means to be unemployed for that period of time, eventually, I will need to re-enter the market or else contemplate standing on the street corner with my hat extended out.

So, the decision I make today will impact my reality one year or so from now. If my calculations are right, that is just about the time when my money will run out.

It is time I get going.

This decision does not stop me from going to the pool, though. If work-life balance cannot be accomplished while on vacation, then we are all doomed.

Saturday November 6

To test my hands at writing, and also to find a medium to channel this drive of mine to write, I have been writing a blog for a little while. True to my troubled mind, though, I have not published it. So, when I say I am writing a blog, it is a bit of a joke because it sits on my hard drive and there alone.

I am torn between publishing it and not; something about the worldwide web intimidates me. I can't write anything pretending it is true when it is not. That is just me. So what I write is true. But, if I want to have a business as a consultant one day, what good will it do me to bare my soul and myself in sharing my fears, doubts, and assorted flaws? It makes me look vulnerable and not always resourceful. I'm not sure those images fit into a business plan!

Since I am dying to share my writing, but too chicken to publish it, I decide to start with a select group of friends, mostly family and close friends, to see what they say. So here I go. Today is my mother's birthday and I decide to launch my blog, off-line. Why today? Because you need a deadline to deliver, and because my mother's birthday is as good as any in the dead of November, when nothing else drives my schedule.

What do I have to say on my blog? Well, it started out as a personal diary. Now, at the onset of this sabbatical, I cannot possibly foresee all that this year will bring; I have been around long enough to know it will be loaded with hurdles, surprises, peaks, and potentially interesting perks of life. Once I am on "the other side" of such peaks and valleys, I want to be able to work my way backward, understand what were the triggers, the wrong turns, the right decisions, and hopefully, draw some lessons from that journey and share them along the way. Since I typically pay no attention to the mundane activities of my life—what city I am in, what date it is, which restaurant I am going to—I tend to have a broken memory at best. Tem is my external memory. He can tell me what I wore on our first date and what I had for dinner. Me? I am lucky if I remember where I parked my car. So, capturing it all in a blog will ensure I don't forget anything.

As it stands, I know when this journey starts, but there is no telling where and when it will end. This blog is intended to track its footprints.

We will see where that will lead. If nothing else, I have found writing it to be a highly efficient hamster sedative. Knocks it right out!

Sunday November 7

I am flying to Montreal today. Again.

The passenger sitting next to me is, at most, twenty-two years old. He has a middle seat. Much to his distress, the screens are not working, so there is no movie today. As far as I can tell, that is a serious issue for him. He is evidently challenged by the prospect of the next five hours.

For the first thirty minutes, he keeps trying to make the screen work, turning it on, off, on again, off again. Finally, he gives up. I guess even he can come to terms with the definition of stupidity!

He pulls out his iPhone, plays some games, fiddles with the magazines in the back-pocket of the seat in front of him, even tries to reach for my back-pocket.

I draw the line.

He twists and turns, tries to sleep for a full ten minutes or so, goes through his entire pack of gum, and finally pulls out his laptop. I am thinking that he is finally going to settle down.

He turns on some action-filled movie where the soundtrack is louder than the music in my earbuds. While watching the movie, he is also playing some games on his iPhone, I suppose to keep him busy for the few nanoseconds when the guys are dead in the movie and the action slows down or something . . . . He is making me dizzy.

I am fairly proficient at multitasking myself, but this is some serious multitasking. Perhaps my thoughts around the benefits of being able to sit still and take in the surroundings are over-rated, but I believe it does everyone some good. It is often thought of as a regenerating moment.

Of course, who needs regeneration at twenty-two?

He reminds me of my firstborn son when he was a preschooler. His energy level was such that I would regularly open the back door of the house and tell him to go run around the yard. "Just bring the energy level down, boy; Mama here can't deal with it no more!"

I feel like doing the same here, but the flight attendant won't let me open the back door!

Tuesday November 9

I wake up, rested and at peace. An unusual state of mind. Then it hits me like a tropical rainfall. I open my eyes and suddenly realize how quiet I am. My body is heavy, comfortable, and rested. I actually had a full night's sleep.

My brain is quiet. My brain is quiet. Did I say that my brain is quiet? The hamster has gone to sleep, maybe even passed out. Who knocked it out?

I did not hear it leave. It is much like falling asleep in a crowded, noisy room, and suddenly waking up when everyone has left and the noise has died. You don't know when it went from chaotic to quiet, but all you know is that the noise is gone.

Now, I want this to last.

Is this it? Did I cross a landmark? Was sixty days the magic number, and now my body and brain can come down a notch and live together in harmony? How many more notches are there?

Reaching this new stage is similar to stepping on a scale after a few weeks of dieting and finding that I have shed a few pounds (although I would not know *that* feeling). It is a sign that I am heading in the right direction.

A great feeling.

My plans for today are to soak in the tub, write, and maybe, just maybe, if I feel that energetic, go for a long walk along the canal. A day off!

I am just settling into my morning routine of coffee and newspaper, and everyone knows how sacred that is, when the phone rings. It is my friend Carla, the business owner I have been helping with a presentation for her new client. We are not ready for tomorrow's presentation.

I jump in the shower, dress, and leave the house, take the subway to Tem's office, borrow the car keys (and the car), and drive across town to her office.

Not quite my idea of a day off, but that's okay. Like I said, she is a friend.

For the first time in nearly three months, I sit in an office, behind a desk, with buzz all around. Honestly, it feels good, so long as I know that tonight I will be heading home and be out of here. Not ready yet.

Wednesday November 10

A real day at the office today. Carla, her associate, and I go over the dry run for the presentation. Then we head out to the client for a two-hour meeting. I feel no pressure or stress. None.

I should have!

Carla is very knowledgeable about her industry and her field. Not only does she master her game, but she has also been hugely successful at it. Her reputation is equal to none. She is my age, bordering on being tired of this pace, and way past the desire to prove herself to newcomers.

The client we are meeting is also represented by three women, each half our age. That, in and of itself, is not an issue. We work with people half our age and even younger all the time. Of course we do; we are nearing retirement!

This client wants bells and whistles, 3-D graphics and statistics, and promises from us to deliver the impossible. These women want a "package" they can wrap and deliver to their own bosses and check off their "To Do" lists. They don't want partnership, working relationships, and all that jazz. They just want the goods.

What we bring to the table is not what they want.

As we stand in the parking lot after the meeting, debriefing, I feel frustrated for Carla. She has to go on working in that environment. I, on the other hand, feel relieved that I don't.

Well, not for now at least. Somewhere, though, in the back of my mind again lurks the thought that, should I elect to become a consultant, I too will have to deal with my own client's expectations and attitude. I may not always escape that easily. After such a break from it all, will I be able to face the music? Will I ever want to do that? I am aware that I currently still entertain the rose-colored spectacles view that I will select clients and mandates. I have a serious attitude when it comes to dealing with people for whom I have no time.

Quite frankly, it's about time I do.

Sunday November 14

As a working executive, there are many days when minutes are sucked into hours, and before you know it, you have been at work for fifteen hours straight. On a good day, you have solved a whole lot of issues. On a not so good day, you have accumulated all sorts of problems and resolved none or next to none!

You are at your computer before sunrise, on the road before the kids are in school, at work until well past sunset, and driving home, you know you will miss the evening news.

Fascinating how on vacation your days are filled with a fraction of that, and yet they feel full and good. Very good.

Tem and I are taking a few days off and driving to Maine to enjoy what we thought would be walks on the beach while the winter sea would forcefully push its cold wind on the coast. Instead, we are able to stretch under the sun and get a bit of suntan as summer is hanging on. Nobody is complaining!

Since my latest epiphany about the joy of writing, I have added a few hours of writing as often as I can to my morning routine. As I sit still and reflect, I realize that, for the better part of my life, I have been making up stories in my head. Now, somehow, I feel the urge to download it all. As I do so, a lot of memories and past events from my life vividly come back to me. As I move forward in life, I discover that, very often, what I experienced as challenges or burdens at one point, become, in time, cherished thoughts. What appeared as critically important is, today, not so relevant, and what appeared insurmountable looks more like a bump in the road.

It is a fascinating twist of events. Perhaps capturing thoughts on paper will give all these memories the credit they deserve. It might also give me the proper perspective.

At the end of the day, other than life and death, and anything leading to either state, not a whole lot out there is as serious as we make it out to be.

Why then would I let anything run or ruin my life? Seriously?

As I reflect on these things, I am sitting in the air terminal waiting for my 6 p.m. flight home to Vancouver. I feel tired. The clock on the street corner shows 10 p.m. when I walk into my condo's lobby. That means 1 a.m. Eastern Time in my body. Today is a long day.

The difference is still tangible between coming home to an empty apartment now that my daughter is gone, and coming home to an empty apartment when she was still living with me but just gone for the night. Now, the first thing to hit me is the smell of the place. It smells like home, but not quite the same. The aroma of her life no longer lingers in the air. There is a stillness hard to describe.

What you leave behind is what you find when you return. Right down to the coffee mug ring on the countertop. Not that she was particularly one to clean up after me while I was gone, but there was always evidence that life had gone on even while I was gone.

No more so.

Monday November 15

This morning, I have a 9 a.m. class with the career transition firm. I love the walk to the office in the early morning. Walking to and from the office has always been my dream. I also wanted to travel the world. So, there you go. You figure it out! Me? I am still searching.

Today, we look at our individual profile. I have completed several of these in my career. This one is quite comprehensive, and not geared toward a specific job, so it is all about me. Not surprisingly, but overwhelmingly, it confirms that my interests, talents, and needs are one and only one: artistic. First and foremost in the literary fields, and then musical in close second.

This result is not a complete surprise. My first love has always been arts, even though I spent my life in the business world. So far I have been unable to blend both, but I am not done yet. Perhaps it is what my daughter was sensing when she asked me, "Mom, when did you stop being a hippie?" Well, what to think of that profile? The obvious option is to be totally depressed and realize that I should have been the ballerina I always dreamed of being, but now it is too late. The other option is to be thrilled because it means a whole new world is out there waiting for me if I take it seriously. This time I am very tempted to. I have time, and should I fall flat on my face, I will be the only one with a broken nose. I am not dragging anybody down with me.

So! How does an HR executive articulate, in her professional arena (because I will need to make a living at one point), her artistic self?

Huh . . . ?

I guess this is my quest. This is the journey I am on.

Wednesday November 17

IT IS BACK! Someone must have left the back door open because it is back. I know so because it kept me up most of the night.

This work with the career transition firm, combined with the time I have on my hands to think, and all that soul-searching, are bringing together all the elements of my life, creating a perfect storm. These elements feel as though they are all looking at me for an answer.

Taking a look at my life was the plan. I am on track. Just slightly unnerved about it all. That's all.

I am not only validating my resume and career path, but also my interests, focus, wants, and dislikes in a manner that, for the first time, I feel really allows me to make a choice. A real choice. There is no other driver than my own needs. This is a new place for me. As I progress in this journey, I find less and less synergy between what I would like to do, and what I have been doing—otherwise referred to as a pickle! This pickle is not totally unexpected, though. So, when it comes to updating a resume, presenting myself on LinkedIn, researching the job market, selecting fields of studies etc . . . two things pop up.

First: an attitude. Basically, I don't want to do this—I don't want to be making plans for my future. I want a break, but I am unable to take a break because I don't know what my future will be. No wonder I feel dizzy.

Second: a major bottleneck. If I knew what I was looking for, it might be easier to find it. Simply put, no job, no income. So, once the severance money runs out, how do I reconcile all of this? Do you truly reinvent yourself at fifty-five, or did I just drink the Kool-Aid?

Yes. I think you can. The smart way to do it, though, is to build on my acquired skills and knowledge of the past and to apply them to my values and passion. Sounds easy on paper, but how I will translate it into a day-to-day activity and a paycheck is another story.

What if I never evolve in the HR arena again? What if I pick up a fruits and vegetables home delivery business? An online order business? Better yet, what if I finally open that proverbial diner where I flip burgers six months out of the year, and flip my buns on the beach for the remaining six?

This is pretty much what my internal hamster and I have been working on all night. This is what it came back for. It could not wait any longer to share it with me.

Friday November 19

In the Career section of *The Globe* today is an article on conversation patterns. The author goes on to explain that conversations must be structured: have a topic, a defined audience, a goal, the whole nine yards. He lists twelve types of conversations and how to lead them: the connector, the influencer, the mediator.

Give me a break! I don't know why I am so on edge these days—maybe from all these career transition classes teaching us all the recipes, formulas, and templates of how to be, what to say, how to look. They get me worked up in no time at all, and this article does that just the same. For most, guidelines are a lot easier to deal with, I will admit. Some people do follow the recipe, line-by-line. I, however, don't.

So, for me, these classes of "how to" are a challenge. A serious one. If you ever tried to put a cat in a tub full of water, then you know what I mean.

Where does this disease of formatting everything come from? Why is it that we find value and comfort in setting rules and tips for everything? I find it most unnerving. Are there people out there so desperate that they need a reference manual to hold a conversation? What is the value of a conversation set on a template?

I have fond memories of how as a child, other than on school days, my days were structured that way: I would wake up to a warm breakfast already set on the table. I would get dressed, and I knew where to find my clothes; neatly folded in my set of drawers. The selection was mine. Then I would go outside and play. When my stomach started growling, it was usually time for a meal. I knew the day had ended, and it was time to come in when the porch-light was on. That's it. This is how much structure we had.

I loved it, and I think I have been longing for that kind of environment ever since I left home to go to grade school. No fancy toys, no already made-up kitchen sets, nursing kits, no on/off switches. We made it all up. Most of the time, all we had were rocks, tall grass, shovels, pails, bicycles, skipping ropes . . . and even that must have been too much given how many times I managed to lose some of the little bit I had.

How my generation became the parents who needed to have a Fisher Price version of everything in life for their kids, I don't know.

So today, when I read about how to have a conversation, I think our children should have gone out and played outside some more.

Once my morning routine is completed, I get dressed, pack my gear, and head out to the airport. I am flying to Montreal this morning. It is -3 degrees and snowing in Vancouver. It is sunny and +6 at my destination. My boots and warm coat are in Montreal, of course (logic would suggest), and I leave home in my shoes and raincoat . . . . It is hard to be always on top of it all!

My time on the plane is spent mostly writing. A good time. I am even frustrated when I hear the engines slow down and feel a slight pitch forward . . . We are nearing destination. Isn't there a holding pattern we can go into?

I enjoy it that much.

Sunday November 21

A leisurely morning for me. Tem and I drove to Ottawa yesterday from the airport. He is attending a conference, and the day is mine until 3 p.m. Sometimes, I struggle with the good life. It is as if I think it will turn into a pumpkin at a given time, much like Cinderella's coach, and leave me on the curb, without so much as a bicycle to get home. Not sure why I think goodness is on a timer.

3 p.m. sharp. I sit in the hotel lobby. 3:05 p.m. Tem shows up. We have a perfect sense of timing. We drive back to Montreal on time to join my children for dinner.

My children are all adults now. They are shaping their own lives. It is hard not to think of them as kids, though. I see them work hard at finding their ways, their happiness. In that quest, as in anything else, it is often two steps forward, one step backward.

The backward one is the hard one to take as a parent. You so much want to help. From the moment your children are born, you don't want them to hurt. That never goes away. You learn to tame this need to help them and hold yourself back, but you are never, ever indifferent to their struggles and pains.

Tonight, I see shadows in one of my sons' eyes, and consequently, it clouds my night a bit.

Monday November 22

I am meeting him (the son with the clouds) today. The plan is to spend the afternoon at the book fair. He suggests we go for coffee first. Now, I know my children love me. They would not miss an opportunity to see me when their schedule allows. However, when they ask to go for coffee or lunch, I know something is rattling up their brain. Today is no exception, and I understand some of the shadow I saw last night.

Three children are like a bird's formation in midair. Each one takes a turn at leading the pack and straggling behind. I guess I should take my lessons from the birds. They never fly in a straight, even line. Things are never equal for everybody. There will always be one who will need a pull.

So we spend more time lunching and talking than we do book browsing. That is okay. Browsing was just the excuse anyway. Besides, I always feel in my element when someone comes up to me for advice. The old HR hat goes back on. Or is this the mother hat? Sometimes, it is hard to differentiate life and work, and sometimes, you just don't need to. They go hand-in-hand.

He walks back to the condo with me. On the way, we stop at the grocery store. He gives me suggestions for dinner, and so it is that Tem comes home to a cooked meal tonight.

The stare on Tem's face when he opens the front door and smells the aroma of a home-cooked meal!

"Don't you get used to this," I say.

Wednesday November 24

You have heard of Pavlov? He trained his dogs to behave in a predictable manner. Something to do with bells and whistles!

My children, my ex, and I have spent twenty years together as a family. We have been out of that family for nearly as many years by now. Tonight, for Philippe's graduation from culinary school, we get together to celebrate, and I am amazed at how the old patterns are ingrained. No matter how much we have evolved since the divorce, it seems that we fall right back into whom we were. At least I do. Is this nostalgia? Subconsciousness? Or is it just a genuine effort to keep everyone comfortable by repeating the familiar patterns? Or maybe nothing at all, and this feeling is all in my head. Not sure. So much goes on in my head.

It feels like running two computers side-by-side, one screening the present and one screening the past, and constantly going back and forth between the two, validating current positions, angles, pressure. A huge strain on my brain! I'm too old for this kind of tension, and mostly, I no longer want to deal with it, and that is a good thing.

After the ceremony, we have cocktails, then dinner. It is a lovely evening. I will always welcome such times when we can be a family again, regardless of how elusive it is.

By the time I drop myself on the backseat of the cab, I have a splitting headache. I should have known that the present is the only place to be.

Thursday November 25

The alarm goes off at 5 a.m. I have an 8 a.m. flight, and I am not packed yet. This time I am heading west. Going back home. Are you keeping track?

I am always happy to get home. Immediately upon arriving, I drop everything in the hallway, change clothes, and head to my career transition class starting at 1 p.m. I have not left the condo yet, but I am already anxious to return. I love the first night back at home.

I should have stayed home after all. Class is depressing today. Eighty percent of entrepreneurs venturing into new businesses fail, they say. Nothing like a pep talk. I profoundly dislike the teacher's attitude. How the heck can she pretend to know what we will encounter and how we will react? She is drawing a gloomy picture of what start-up entrepreneurs face when they get out there, and although I know she is right, statistically, I don't want to hear it. Don't you tell me what my world will be before I have a chance to step into it. My world isn't yours and that is also a good thing!

I am not a happy camper. I feel like walking up to her and saying, "Let me tell *you* where *you* are going to be two years from now. *You* will be exactly where you are today. *You* ain't going nowhere with that attitude!"

She makes me feel like a loser among many! My walk home is invigorating. That's for sure.

The only thing on my agenda for the rest of the day is Wings with Ed. I normally drive since this is one of the rare occasions I have to take the car. This time, however, I take the SkyTrain on account of the ten centimeters of snow Vancouver just covered itself under. Vancouverites do not deal well with snow.

Today is also the American Thanksgiving. I have learned to love that holiday. Not that I celebrate it. As Canadians, we have our own. However, I learned to love it because all my American colleagues did, and at last, for one day, the email traffic slowed down, and I could have some peace and quiet!

My days are still so full I don't get around to doing everything I want to. Proof is, my piano is still collecting dust. A few things have changed, though. For one, my email traffic is considerably reduced. So are my phone calls. In fact, some days, were it not for Brooks Brothers, Barnes & Noble, and Air Canada promotional emails, I would not receive any.

I feel funny in saying this; there is almost a sense of shame attached to that statement. As you know, in the workplace, email traffic has become akin to a popularity contest. At the water cooler, in the elevator, people talk about relentless email traffic the way they used to talk about the weather. Typically, the worse the weather, the better the conversation. So it goes with email. So, to admit that your email traffic has died is a statement requiring a strong dose of self-confidence.

Being unemployed is a professional challenge. Being unemployed with low email traffic, a social challenge. A potent combination.

In the end, Ed and I cancel. The roads are a mess. He can't make it to the bar either. I head out to the gym instead. The best thing about Vancouver, besides the breathtakingly beautiful scenery, and the weather (most of the time), is that I can put on my leggings, my big heavy boots, winter coat, pink mittens, and a green scarf, and head out to the gym with my hair in a ponytail, and think nothing of it. I know for a fact that no one else will either! We just do our thing. No fashion consciousness here.

Now that my daughter is no longer here to tell me, "Mom, did you intend to go out dressed like this, or did you just forget to change?" I think sometimes I may be slightly over the top.

When it comes time to turn the lights out and go to sleep, I am grateful for my workout. It did me some good. I can tell my sleep will benefit from it.

Just as I reach out for my phone to turn it off, I get a text message from Julie.

"Mom, it's urgent! What is a tragic opera with a very well-known melody?"

"THAT is urgent? What do you need to know this for?"

"I need this for classes tomorrow morning. I have two minutes to sing an excerpt, and for people to recognize it."

Don't you love your kids? If I am getting ready to turn in for the night, granted I go to bed early; this means it is way past her bedtime being that she is on the East Coast. And she is looking for this now? Tragic opera? My first thought is Mozart's *Don Giovanni*. Hardly appropriate for the petite redhead beauty she is. Then I am thinking

Wagner, Verdi, Puccini; problem is tragic is not always popular. She has thirty seconds to make it stick. I am also thinking that Cinderella is a better character for hcr. What can I say? I am the Mom. To me, she is a princess.

By the time I reply with my suggestion, her phone is off. So who is the smart one here? My lights go out.

Friday November 26

It is raining today. Everyone is happy. Things are back to normal. The snow is gone.

I am tired. I sit in class and am struggling with concentration. My left eye is twitching, usually an undeniable sign of fatigue. How can I be tired? I have been off work for nearly three months now. Why tired? I don't know. Perhaps it is this perpetual management of the "To Do" list? Amazing how this list has an endless quality to it. The more I cross off its top, the more it grows out from the bottom. Much like your email, wouldn't you say? Or the debit column of my checking account!

Seems to me like it will be months before I am ready to hit the road and start earning an income. By then, a chunk of my money will be gone. What if I run out? What if I don't make enough to afford the lifestyle I want? What if I can't establish myself in both cities and have to decide between the two? What if? What if?

Exhausting.

This is one of those "Life is a bitch and then you die" days. I should have stayed in bed this morning. A lot of what tires me is the sense of not making progress. I feel stationary in my life and these same questions come back again and again and worse, remain unanswered. I know. It is all in my head. I get that.

When I get home, it is already dark outside. I am leaving tomorrow, again, for the weekend.

This schedule is starting to get to me. So much of me wants everything. The balance is the struggle here. So tonight, I turn everything off, including my brain, and go to bed early.

Brain and body are like an old couple. They have ways of getting along and knowing when to take turns at being the lead, most of the time. So, as I go to bed, my body is in the driver's seat and everything is quiet. We appear to be in for a good night.

Not for long. By 3 a.m., my brain cannot hold still any longer. "Move over" it tells my body and takes the lead. They argue for a while, much like a dancing couple fighting over who leads. The body yields. The brain takes over. I cannot go back to sleep.

A predictable scenario!

It is now 4 a.m. Coffee aroma fills the apartment. I am already into section two of the *Globe & Mail*. The news is depressing. I think I need to stop reading and thinking. Perhaps I need to sign up for some lighter activities such as tap dancing, a beer drinking contest, or knitting. I don't know. I need to lighten up.

Of course I am on time at the airport.

I get to Montreal late in the afternoon with just enough time to go home, change, and meet a couple of Tem's friends for dinner. Tomorrow will be a true day off.

A short but sweet weekend.

Tuesday November 30

Nine hours of uninterrupted sleep. If I were not in a serious relationship, I would say this is better than sex!

My dream is still fresh in my mind. I am telling my friends, real friends I can recognize, that I know I am not ready to go back to work because I am still short-tempered. Then one of them turns to me, and says, "Maybe you will never be ready to go back."

I am worried. Is that what is really bugging me? They say that dreams manage the subconscious part of your life that you need to deal with but won't. So, am I worried I will not want to go back to work?

Damn right I am. Surely, I did not need a dream to tell me that. I believe I could always land a job. I am just not sure I will want to. At least, not the types of jobs I have had in the past. So, really, I am still on track with the original plan, and maybe that is not so bad. I know I need to reinvent my job. This much I know, and it is not new news.

What is new is my becoming aware of everything out there I am interested in. Perhaps knowing that so much is possible makes it all come to life in a more meaningful way? Before, it did not matter whether or not these options were there; I was not stopping to contemplate any of them! In time, I will have to decide: Not going back to my established career and seeking to find my dream job is just a spoiled brat's fancy life illusion, or it is fundamentally what I need to do—assuming I find what that is! Secretly, and with a certain amount of embarrassment, I must admit that all this navel-gazing comes with a certain level of guilt and discomfort. Hard to explain.

First, from the time you are a young child, you are trained not to be idle. "Go out and play; don't just sit there!" In adulthood, this translates into "Go get yourself a job. Don't just stand there!" and once you have one, it is "Don't you have work to do?"

So, a lot of it does not come naturally. I am hoping it will get better.

Another meeting with my career transition coach today. I want to review my plans with her, discuss my progress so far, and also put the program on hold starting mid-December.

Her office is overheated, my expectations overrated, so I hastily conclude the meeting and get out of there. Some places are just not where you are meant to be at that moment. It is just not in me to share my plans before I am ready to execute them. Besides, she is suggesting a whole series of steps and actions I am not planning on dealing with at this stage.

Instead, I make plans to meet with a business contact in Montreal over the holidays as well as another one here in Vancouver, as early as next week. I am still fishing.

Finally, this career transition thing will probably end up like everything else in my life. I will do it by myself, my own way!

I am beginning to think I may have an attitude.

Thursday December 2

I am flying to . . . Toronto today. Tricked you! I should be happy since I have three nice days ahead of me, but instead, I am in a crappy mood. Remnants of yesterday, I should think. Sometimes, even pleasant is difficult when you take it from the wrong angle.

On my way to catch the bus to the train station to get to the airport (you can see what mood I am in), my purse's shoulder-strap snaps, and

I enter the bus with a purse, a briefcase, a suitcase, and a handful of change in my hands, battling a lineup of people trying to make their own way in an already crowded bus.

I miss the days of riding in a cab. Sometimes, being green does not come naturally either.

I make it to the airport on time. Boarding is slow. The flight is full. The passenger next to me won't shut up. Not dealing well with life's irritants today.

The journey from Toronto airport to downtown, at 5:30 p.m. on a Thursday, is exactly that: a journey. First, I find out there is no shuttle bus to the hotel. I should have known that. I have to take public transit. Nothing wrong with that when you know where you are going.

I don't.

One needs the exact change to get on the bus. Something else I did not know. Back into the terminal to get change. Standing in line to pay for a bottle of water I have no intention of carrying with me (but they won't give me change unless I buy something), I see my bus go by. Things that I once knew mechanically when I was on a tight budget have become something of the past over the years. When you travel on corporate business, you never wait for the bus, wait in line, or look for change other than for tipping. How quickly we forget.

It is a cold night. I wish I had worn my gloves. I wait a little longer, and freeze a little deeper.

Then I ride the whole distance from the airport to the first subway station, standing up in the middle of the bus, holding on to my suitcase, my briefcase, and probably my life, for all I know, given the way the driver operates.

Finally, once in the subway station, there is no direction stating eastbound our westbound. Of course, there is not. This train only goes east, but I do not know that either as I frantically rush in to catch the train. I jump into the first wagon I see. Enough already! It ought to take me somewhere!

I sit through fifteen consecutive stations, never knowing whether I am on the right train until finally my station is called. I get off.

Technically, the hotel is just a few steps away . . . so they tell me. Well, if that is the case, this hotel is underground, or I am walking in the wrong direction.

I call Tem.

"What does the hotel look like?"

"Where are you?" he asks.

"I don't know. Somewhere on Bloor, between two vacant lots."

"Sweetheart, there are no vacant lots in Toronto."

"Then I must be somewhere else," I snap back. He is a patient and understanding man.

"Turn around and tell me what you see."

I turn on my feet. "One odd looking building leaning over the street."

"Walk in that direction. The hotel is just across the street from it."

And so I do. Within minutes, I step out of the cold into a warm, cozy, luxurious interior, and that sets the tone for the rest of the weekend.

Don't you wish your life could be like that? Just stepping out of the cold into warm and cozy?

Sunday December 5

During the weekend, we take in as much of the city as we can. I have not been back here in a good number of years. Toronto is where I first learned English in my early teens, spending summers as a live-in nanny trying to keep four children well-fed, out of trouble, and ultimately, alive while their parents were on the tennis court, at the beach, or simply reading in the backyard.

I loved going away for the summer.

As the day darkens and the dampness of night moves in, the walk back to the hotel through the University of Toronto campus is remarkably peaceful and pleasant. Although neither one of us was ever a student here, it feels like a trip down memory lane.

It is now Sunday and time to go home. We hit the movies at noon to catch the first showing. Then, we jump into a cab and head out to the airport. Since we have plenty of time, we end the weekend in comfortable chairs in the lounge, sipping a last glass of wine.

On the way to our respective gates, the Sunday afternoon blues hit. The sun is setting already. The terminal is quiet, somewhat dark, and people are just walking in line. A total sense of submission is in the air. I had forgotten how heavy Sunday nights can feel. A lot of these people are already positioning for the beginning of the week. Their weekends are over already.

We part at the gate. I go west; he heads east. In this country, we call this the two solitudes.

Long distance relationships are great when you reunite. They are just not so hot when you are heading back home.

By the time, I get home it is 11 p.m. local time. As usual, unless I am dead tired, I always unpack. That way I already feel at home when I get up the next day.

In doing so, I realize I have left my laptop AC adaptor on the plane.

I knew I was missing something when we deplaned, but I could not think what it was. It was less than one hour ago when I exited that plane, and with any luck, it is still at the gate, waiting for its turnaround, or so I think. I want to talk to someone in the terminal—the cleaning crew perhaps, the ground crew manager—someone must have found it, or else it is simply at my seat, still warm, standing in solitary abandonment. It is my cord, no, not the umbilical but almost. Please, I need this!

I am instructed to contact the online service desk and open a ticket with Adesh in Bangalore, India. The agent gives me a reference file number and informs me that the airline has ninety days to find it or close the ticket.

Sounds to me like, "Don't call us; we'll call you."

Globalization is overrated!

Monday December 6

This entire day is intended to be a day off. I know I keep saying that. It is because I keep trying to feel like I am on vacation.

No class, no lunch, no appointment, totally free, and the plan is to make it day one of my thirty day, yet again, yoga extravaganza (I am still trying.) But the first two hours are spent trying to locate an AC adaptor for my laptop. No, it is not as simple as walking up to Future Shop and buying one. Even I had thought of that.

The model I bought is "particular," the manufacturer says. Particular is not necessarily what I would use to describe my mood. Because it is "particular," even the universal model that fits "all types" (except mine, of course), does not fit. You'd think they would tell you how "particular" it is when you buy it. I sure don't recall having had that conversation!

So the manufacturer has a single warehouse in Canada, and it is in Ontario. Roughly a five-day drive from here! Of course, he offers to mail it. The first section (the adaptor) is available and I can have it in one week. The other section, the cord, is not available. It will be another ten to fifteen days before I get it.

I'd say this is consistent with my expectations!

Forget the manufacturer. I am sure I can find clones somewhere. I go on eBay, visit craigslist, call my friends, and have them beg their IT departments to find a compatible cord. Nothing works. I call my technician. I am hoping he will have more clout than me in bribing someone to find me one, but regrettably, he does not. Meanwhile, I revert to working on my home PC, the type you need to crank up manually (almost!) with an older version of everything, a much slower processor, and a wobbly keyboard.

While I want this period of my life to be meaningful and enlightening, I find myself spending more time than I care to admit, on stupid, useless, time-consuming, energy-draining mindless activities. How do I prevent them from infiltrating my life? How did I not have these before? Was someone else dealing with them? Is this what money bought me? If so, then this situation is a truly compelling argument for keeping my corporate job!

I need to shake this frustration off if I want to enjoy the rest of my day. I will not let it change my plan. I am going to yoga first. A brisk forty-minute walk and I am at the studio. I have not done hot yoga in nearly six months. As expected, it is brutal.

Trying to determine when is the best time to work my body, or my brain, remains difficult. I went to hot yoga class once on a full stomach. Never again! You would not think that your stomach has anything to do with your ability to stretch your muscles, but believe me, it does, and if you don't believe me, I suggest you ask a friend. Don't try it on your own unless you don't mind looking at your lunch spilled all over your yoga mat while you are coming down into plank! Scheduling is everything. It seems that whatever I do in the morning is the only thing that gets all the attention it deserves. After that, the day takes over and it is all downhill from there. It is always a battle.

It reminds me of when my dad was still driving but had started being uncomfortable with traffic. He was planning his errands so he did not have to be on the road before 10 a.m., making sure he returned before 2 p.m., and preferably avoided the lunch hour traffic. So, with any luck, he had time to go to the post office and back.

Maybe my life has become too small, I am thinking; and this is telling me it is time I get a little more action going.

Thursday December 9

Ninety days have gone by since I stopped working. This is more time off than I ever had in my entire career, with the exception of when my ex and I were both laid off from the same company after it went belly up! Since we had a mortgage, three kids, a dog, and more worries than we cared to deal with, it hardly felt like time off.

So, this time is a novelty. At the onset of a sabbatical, ninety days seems like a long stretch, during which you will have plenty of time to do all the things on your "To Do" list. On the morning of the ninetieth day, however, it does not feel like such a long time at all, and that "To Do" list looks like it has barely been touched. If anything, it seems to have grown longer.

So what have I accomplished? I feel the need to check because it does not feel like I have done much. Maybe I am wrong.

Just off the top of my head, I can say that my finances and my house are in order. My Montreal condo is furnished and rented. I have established that I will not seek employment in the corporate arena in the near future, and potentially, ever. I have become autonomous; actually, that may be a stretch; let's settle with becoming almost autonomous, with my mobile apparels (laptop, BlackBerry, Internet providers etc.) and my renewed frequent flyer status for another year.

What is also worth mentioning are the numerous walks in the woods, laps at the pool, rollerblading and bike spins around the sea wall, as well as catching up with most of my friends, and realizing how much I had missed all of these activities, and how valuable they are. I also took a nice vacation to Europe. There is no smooth way to ease out of the workforce. It is a brutal event. So dropping everything and leaving for vacation was totally appropriate. Then I applied and was accepted to university (again) and attended at least half of the career transition classes for which I registered.

I have also been known on my good days to cook. Occasionally.

I have returned to yoga (just barely though), and last but not least, have started writing a blog and discovered how much I like it.

So, overall, not bad for a girl who just wanted to be on vacation. However, I do not believe I have resolved the core issue. It still feels like what I want to do does not tie up with earning an income. Most of the time, that is. Of course, I will have to find that piece of the puzzle one day, but for now, it is nowhere to be found, and I am getting edgy. I need a mission, a purpose. I am working really hard at keeping the thread here. I want to see results. I want to cross things off my list, and to have a sense of accomplishment.

Since I have made no progress in the career area, I feel my most tangible work is my writing.

Now I want to share it in a big way. I am anxious to know whether I am writing this for the recycling bin, or whether someone, other than my mother, will actually be interested in reading it one day, so the closed circle of friends as sole readers does not suffice anymore.

How will I ever be able to share it? I don't mean what tool I should use. That is not where the trouble lies. I don't know "how," meaning where will I find the courage and boldness to share publicly all my inner fears, doubts, warts, and all? Not that I am embarrassed by anything I say; on the contrary, I kind of like what I say. It is mostly that I just think I am not your typical boardroom conversation, and that may be detrimental to my aspirations of going out there as a consultant or a coach. That scares me. I have a sixth sense telling me to be careful, and I am trying to find out whether it is genuine or simply a gross impostor. So much digging and soul-searching. Now I know why people drink.

For now, I am off to yoga. It is the middle of the day and pouring rain. I am walking along Nelson Street. My iPod covers the street sounds. Rain is running down my face, and I love it. I feel light, connected, and everywhere I look, I like what I see.

Does this mean I am ready to go back to work? Why do I keep asking that question? What if I just enjoyed where I am at?

I take the SkyTrain to New Westminster and join a friend for cocktail hour after class. I get there early and sit at the bar. It suddenly hits me that it is the holiday season. Office parties are in every corner;

wrapping paper is all over the floor; Christmas carols are in the background music, and waiters are wearing deer antlers.

Good God! Where have I been all this time? Now that my days are not tracked to the fifteen-minute interval, I seem to have lost the notion of time. Have we come to the end of the year?

Friday December 10

Today is the last day of the week meant to be dedicated to writing. So far, I have only covered fifteen pages of my book.

I am totally down on myself for what appears to be a lack of progress. It seems like all I do is search the Internet, wait on line, fix server connections, wait for the mail, upload and download countless data, search for tutorials on all the endless new apps, update documents, etc. I feel like a chicken with its head cut off. I am going in all directions but heading nowhere, busy doing meaningless things, which, I am convinced, only I do not know how to do. I am sure others can do them all with their eyes closed and their fingers up their noses.

Of course, it is convenient to think that way. Feeling sorry for myself is a very cozy fallback position. It allows me to stall. In fact, the anxiety is not only about what to do with my writing, but also and mostly about what to do with the reality that I am heading toward starting my own business, and I need to get organized, become visible, profitable, and all that jazz. Besides, this is all so, so, lonely. No IT department, no onboarding, no secretary, no advisory board or team, just me. So, why plan to write when what I need to do is work on business development?

Well, that question touches the heart of every single dilemma in my life. The struggle between doing what I like and doing what I ought to be doing, and why the hell, for the life of me, can't I get to a place where the two are the same? I don't know. At this point, I have developed an attitude. I will stick to doing what I want. We'll see where that will take me.

Enough of that.

Being that we are a week away from Christmas, something else is on my mind.

Tem and I have a black tie dinner next week. This is sweet except that the last time I went to such a dinner, it was summer, so the dress won't work. Then, the time before that, I was still slim and slender . . . so that dress won't work either! (Why I keep it in a box under my bed with hope that it will fit me one day is not entirely clear). God, I hate shopping! Why is it that there is always something I need?

I hit the stores with as much enthusiasm and energy as one can display on the way to the dentist. And then it gets worse. It would appear that I am still suffering from a severe case of distortion when it comes to sizing a dress that fits me. Totally depressed, exhausted, and defeated, I am heading back home, no bags in tow, wondering whether lululemon stretch pants are an acceptable alternative to a cocktail dress at a black tie dinner. They are black after all.

Then, something catches my eye in a display window. I enter the store, and before I know it, the saleslady has been so skillful and patient in helping me make a selection that she actually sells me a dress, which I might add, suits me well. My self-esteem shoots right back up, and my mood goes in the same direction.

A remarkable recovery.

Almost immediately, I feel guilty for feeling so bad over such trivial stuff. I know I can hold my own in a crowd, meaning I can still catch some looks, but I am nostalgic of how I used to look, and how easy it was to look that way. I am equally upset that it all changed on me, only because I turned fifty, as if that alone were not enough. It's not like I went out on a binge every night. I liked it much better when how I looked depended on what I ate, how much exercise I crammed into my schedule, and how many hours of sleep I got. These days, none of that makes any difference. My body is acting like a teenager. Totally out of control.

Saturday, December 11

For the last five years, I have been trying to figure out whether my sleep pattern and waistline erratic behaviors are related to my age, my job, my mental state, or all of the above. I just don't know. All I know is that I miss the days when they were low profile and simply played along without calling for any attention.

Last night was another poor night's sleep. My brain wanted to know what I will do when I grow up, and it wanted to know right then and there. Yet again.

For some reason, brains are like newborns. They are quiet most of the day, but they run amuck after midnight. The good thing about babies is that *they* grow up and eventually learn to align with the rest of the world (mostly!). Not sure when brains learn to do that.

So this morning, I am upset. I sit down at my computer and retrieve my balance sheet. I review scenarios one, two, three, etc., until I have considered all options (I say review because this is not the first time my brain and I go through this process). I find that pulling numbers is an excellent brain comforter—when the numbers add up that is. In my case, if I want to, I can take years before going back to work. I may even have the option of not going back. Some of these options, of course, require some tough decisions, mostly around where I live. But nonetheless, having options is having possibilities.

So, there! Back off, neurotic brain, and let me do this my own way!

All this financial planning takes the better part of my morning. That time was dedicated to writing initially. See? I've been tricked again. That is how a twisted brain works; somewhat like an addiction. The behavior it draws you toward is not the one you should engage in.

Just to prove it wrong, I summarize my options, post them on my board, turn off my computer, and aim for the gym.

How is that for a diversion?

Sunday December 12

It is the middle of the night and the rain outside sounds like a running faucet in a basin full of water. This is some serious raining. With my eyes closed, I rest my head back and enjoy the sound. All is quiet except for the rain, and my brain. Nevertheless, it is soothing. I like the rain. Maybe it is why I enjoy Vancouver so much. Hard to like this city if you can't stand the rain.

This entire day is intended for running errands and tying loose ends. A feel-good kind of day because there is no rush, and I am not trying to do anything else. One thing at a time. It is shortly after six when I return home. I don't think I will ever tire of owning my Sunday nights now that I am on sabbatical and they are actually mine. Going to bed knowing that tomorrow is mine, as well, is luxury!

Thursday December 16

Only two more days of transition classes. When I return from the holidays, I will be busy with university and with seriously starting to put my thoughts and plan together to ease my way back into the workforce.

Enough thinking. Time to move into action.

At this stage, I have a pretty solid idea of my professional life inventory; what I know, have, can, and wish to pursue. I also know pretty much what I do not have and must acquire. What is left now is to go after it. That is the plan for the new year. I will start with going back to school.

I am happy with where I am, and looking ahead, the immediate future looks quite good. It is the holidays! Friends, family, food, and fun!

What is there not to love?

Friday December 17

Early start today. I go through the morning paper, and a few chapters of my book. I check my email, manage my LinkedIn, balance my checkbook, start the laundry, hem my pants, and make soup before I even leave for class. Class is great today. There are only three of us, and the discussions are very dynamic. I wonder what job would pay me to think and debate all day. That would be a suitable job indeed!

Tuesday December 21

It is still early. I am up and packing. Heading home for the holidays—east that is.

When I get to the airline counter, I am told my seat had to be changed. Whatever. And try as she did, the gate agent could not find me another business seat. No worries. At least I have an aisle seat. It turns out to be a "hot" seat.

Picture the seating arrangement on the plane: Six seats abreast; three on each side of the aisle. A young couple with a teenager (a brother or cousin I am guessing,) and a two-year-old are on my row. The mother asks the teenager to sit with the young child next to a traveler, while the couple sits next to me. All in the same row.

So, starting from the window, you have: baby, teenager, stranger, aisle, me, mother, and father.

What's wrong with this picture?

I am a mother of three. I totally get this. The parents are hoping to get a break and leave the teenager to take care of the child. However, as with everything else in life, there are appropriate places and times for breaks.

An Airbus 320, four days before Christmas, isn't one of them. I can assure you of that.

Sure enough, as we start taxiing, the child starts crying, the teenager panics, the father unbuckles and stands up, shouting instructions to the teenager, and the flight attendant is charging down the aisle. Oh, joy! This is going to be a jolly ride. Since there are four of them, and only two of us strangers, changing seats does not really improve the scenario. So they play "Who wants that kid?" for five hours. Sometimes, the mother takes the child and tries to "plug" her: candies, movie, chips, cookies, and when none of that works, she is totally at a loss what to do with the child. No storybooks, no toys, no singing a song, no braiding hair, nothing.

What happened to motherhood? Honestly, I have never witnessed such a disengaged mother/child relationship.

The father seems to do a better job, although that is debatable. His way of taking care of his child is to tickle her until she is blue in the face and screaming at the top of her lungs. It keeps her busy all right, but it does not afford any of us any rest. In any case, he only has her for a very short while. He seems to prefer the movie.

Wouldn't we all?

And then, to top it all off, we are privileged to witness a kicking, screaming, twirling, blanket-trashing hell of a scene. Twice, actually. I have never seen anything like it. None of us on that row had anything to eat or drink for the entire duration of the flight. We were a designated high risk area.

At long last, we land. As we stand in the aisle waiting for the doors to open in a "Can't wait to get out of Dodge" attitude, the father leans toward the mother:

"This sure was a boring flight," he says.

_____!

The only reason why the father does not wear the imprint of my five fingers across his face as he deplanes is because we start moving, and he is ahead of me.

Timing is everything!

Friday December 24

It is Christmas Eve. In my family, we go to Midnight Mass, then come home at 1 a.m. to open presents and eat. Of course, we eat. We do it first with the immediate family, then with the extended family, and then with friends. It goes on for a few days.

This year, my gift to myself is that I will not think about work, career, consulting vs. corporate world, LinkedIn, blogging, university, tuition fees, or networking for the duration of the holidays. I am off. I am reading fiction, sleeping in, eating, drinking, and being merry. My kind of plan.

As do most people, we exchange gifts with loved ones. There is nothing you can offer my parents as presents, though. They have had it all, and they don't like to collect stuff anymore. So, I give them a printed copy of my blog so far. Although my dad could read it online, my mother would not.

Their feedback comes as a surprise. They claim to be discovering a side of me they had not seen before. My mom and dad? A side of me they do not know? They took me from diapers to the altar! How can there be a side of me they have not seen before?

I find this feedback interesting really. I do not think I am revealing any consequential secrets here. In fact, it is a mere reflection of my day-to-day life. What's inner about that? Perhaps I share more of myself through writing than I do talking? This is highly possible. I am not much of a talker. I am wondering, though. If the people closest to me do not know all of me, what do I know of them? All of a sudden, I wonder whether everyone is a stranger, including myself! What if that hidden side is invisible even to me? How will I ever see it?

I sense a headache coming on . . . .

Tuesday December 28

A cold sub-zero temperature kind of day. The kind that is nicer from the inside looking out. Perfect! I love those. Tem builds a fire; we are not going anywhere. I am just sitting and daydreaming. My hamster is out cold, so all is quiet in my head.

The wrappings and empty boxes from Christmas night are still in the hallway, by the door. They need to make their way to the recycling bin in the basement. I guess that means we will have to pick them up! Again this year, no housecleaning robot was under the tree!

As my eyes rest on them, the memory of my childhood's best-ever Christmas gift pops up: a heavy cardboard box, the type used for ski boots, or skates. That box, once wrapped and nestled under the tree, was stripped from its original content and filled with scissors, ink, paint, glue, paper of all colors, crayons, strings, pads, all kinds of materials to craft with.

More than the dolls, the trendy clothes, or the favorite board game, that box was, by far, the most exciting gift I ever had. It did not contain scissors and crayons and paper; it contained possibilities—trips, clouds, streams, and horses. It was a magic box. Opening it was akin to rubbing the genie's lamp, knowing I could make anything come out of it. To this day, I remember even the smell of it.

I bet my mother never had a clue what an empty Bauer's skates box could mean. To think that she may have wished she could afford to buy me the latest and greatest gadget of the time, whatever that may have been.

There you go! Sometimes, you make your best moves and are not even aware of it.

Friday December 31

As the year ends, Tem and I join friends in Quebec City for what has now become a traditional New Year's Eve dinner, where good food, good music, and great company are the main components. With time, you need less people, less noise, and less booze. People think it is a sign of age, but I beg to differ. It is because we just feel fuller, as in more fulfilled, all around.

Champagne is corked at midnight. We will always need that.

Looking back is comforting. So is looking forward.

PART IV

Don't judge each day by the harvest you reap
but by the seeds you plant.

Robert Louis Stevenson

Monday January 10

Okay. Time's up! This is the New Year; it will be four months tomorrow that I have been on sabbatical. Time to start putting a plan together and earning an income again.

To that end, I have sorted out a few things: I am going back to school with the plan to start my own business as an executive coach, and I will live and work in both Vancouver and Montreal. I will seek help and stop doing everything by myself. I will push through my fears and move ahead even when I don't feel ready to do so. As for cooking, we will see.

Making plans, thinking big, seeing opportunities—this is all the fun stuff. Boiling this down to a paycheck is the true talent.

First thing I get this morning is an email from a recruiting firm in Vancouver asking me to consider an executive HR opportunity.

Is this the trick on every first day of every new resolution? Do I need to be challenged that way on day one? Come on!

I want an executive HR position like a teenager wants a curfew. Do I miss the deadlines, the pressure, the commuting, the here-you-see-it-now-you-don't horizon, the lack of time, workload, and endless crisis? Hell, no!

Do I miss the strategic thinking, the visionary discussions, the conflict resolution, the let's-get-our-heads-together-and-solve-this, the can-you-help-me-work-this-through? Oh, yeah!

Did I make a commitment to myself to find time to write, to focus mainly on areas of my expertise I loved more than others, to stay fit, and to have a life? Yes!

Did I decide to establish myself in both cities so I could keep alive all the loves of my life, namely Tem, family, friends, and Vancouver? Yes!

So, an HR executive position that will tie me to a desk, sixty hours a week in a single location, I figure, matches my needs like a square peg fits in a round hole.

Why do I need to run through the pros and cons, and remind myself of this regularly? I am not sure. Lack of conviction perhaps? The guilt around wanting it all? Might very well be. I still don't answer the email just yet. I will hold on to it for a little bit, just in case. It feels safe—a rare commodity these days. Instead, I get ready for an upcoming meeting with the friend of a colleague of a friend. Networking they call it.

I use these meetings mostly to find out how others do what they do. How their businesses came about, what worked or did not, etc. Finding out about the down-to-earth reality of the project you see as a dream is particularly humbling. It is like deciding to lose ten pounds. It is easy when all you see is yourself in a size six pair of jeans. Once you fully understand the true distance between you and those jeans, then you pay respect.

Meeting with a retired executive coach, former partner to an executive search firm, has that sobering effect.

My first thoughts are that this starting my own business as an executive coach, at this time in my career, is probably bigger than me. The distance between where I am today, which is not even really at the start line, and where I need to get seems way too big. The Great Wall of China is shorter than that, I am sure. The way I am seeing this today, there is no way I can embark on this path.

I said I was going to push through my fears. I did not think I was going to encounter them so early, however. Fears are just thoughts in my head. I know that already. I just need to let that thought come and go. This is when my hamster invites its friends over to make more noise. I am not listening.

Tuesday January 11

A few weeks ago, and against my self-doubting mind, I had contacted someone here in Vancouver to discuss potential board directorship opportunities. I know the drill one has to go through to be considered for board positions, and I recognize it is not the road I traveled. I did it to follow up on a conversation I had with a recruiter who had mentioned that boards are desperately seeking to hire female members, and people with HR background, as well. I thought with a score of two out of two, I might stand a chance!

I had not heard back from them, and assumed, as I typically would, that they took one look at my bio and went: What? Seriously? The nice surprise for me today is that they replied and are suggesting we meet. I am thinking they are interested; at a minimum, they are curious.

What I also find out in going through my email is that my executive coaching program starts on Monday (I knew that), and I need to get some equipment (I did not know that), including a headset and a webcam so I can take the courses online.

A chill runs down my spine. I will have to go shopping again.

As for that executive search in Vancouver, I decline.

Sunday January 16

My plans are all screwed up because it is nice and sunny today. I want to go out and play. I had been counting on rain, so I could get ahead in my reading. However, when the sun shines in Vancouver, you drop everything and head outdoors.

I can play outside while my brain works on projects. Running will do that. The latest project being tossed around in my head is the idea of creating a website. Everybody says I need a website, especially since I don't have a brick-and-mortar place of business. I don't know about that. I've resisted the idea for a long time. It seems like another opportunity to spend hours behind the screen instead of out in the world where, really, my business is. I need to be able to refer people to something other than my business card, I am told, to let them know I exist. Okay. I can try to find some excitement in a website project. I can look at it as if it were a craft project; colors, design, shapes, music maybe . . . I feel like a kid with my Prismacolor box of crayons, except that what I see in my head, I am unable to reproduce on the screen. Since I am as familiar with building a website as I am with molecular biology, I will need to do a whole lot of research or depend on someone else to do it.

I am thinking that I had promised myself to seek help and try to stay away from doing it all myself. This may be the perfect opportunity to see whether I can walk my talk.

Monday January 17

It is back-to-school day today. Day one of the executive coaching program at Royal Roads University on Vancouver Island. Everything about this program sounds sexy. The subject, the location, and the venue (you need to take the ferry to get to it). Even the thought of getting a schedule is exciting. I am expecting assignments, reading material, a calendar, events, and all that good stuff I never thought I would miss so much. Instead, all I find is one big heap of confusion and trials and tribulations while trying to surf the university's site, access all modules, online training etc . . . . Oh, joy!

I never thought I would say this, but I am now grateful for the similar moments I experienced at my previous job. Working globally while your boss, your secretary, and your staff are all in different countries has its challenges at first, but today, I am glad to be familiar with these tools because there is no running down the hall to get help here, and the sooner you make peace with that, the better. The challenge with such an environment is that mostly you are on your own. There is no one at the end of the video to talk to. You cannot ask questions; nor can you find the tutorial typically. Evidently, getting past the identification and password will be a challenge since that information resides in a previous email you did not pay attention to, but if you are lucky, have not deleted yet. Then, once you are well into the site, your screen will freeze. Luckily, there is always a help desk somewhere that you can call for help, but usually, its attendants are in a different time zone, and they typically start their day slightly after you have ended yours.

But don't worry; everyone gets used to it.

Sunday January 23

Last week, I started classes online, but today, I am heading for the campus. I have a week on-site where I will meet students and professors. I am not too sure how I feel. Not as excited as I thought I would. Part of me is scared to death that I will be disappointed and find I have invested time and money into something I will not like. But who knows? No point deciding what it will be before I get there.

Off I go to Vancouver Island. We dock around 7 p.m. It is pitch black and raining cats and dogs. The roads are under construction. I hate driving in the dark. I am alone. Just me and my Google map. I get on campus and find myself more at a loss here than I was on the highway. The directions have no rhyme or reason, and anyway, there are no directions on campus. I end up finding the students' residence, unloading the car, dragging everything up six floors, down two, and across the building—it is an old building. Then I make my way back to the car and drive to the parking lot—a mere mile away!

Walking the trail back from the parking lot (and hoping it is the right trail, because trails, like roads, have no directions here), I quickly realize I did not bring my rain boots nor my umbrella. I thought I would be driving everywhere. What was I thinking? This is BC! We are tree-huggers. If there is a possibility that your car will be made useless, it will. Mind you, this is part of the reason why I love it here, though. So, I'm not complaining, just frustrated and wet! How did I not think to bring rain gear?

After encountering two deer, a raccoon, and a lost peacock, I find myself in the castle's backyard (yes, there is a castle on campus), overlooking the gardens. On a warm sunny Sunday morning, I would bet this is beautiful. On a dark, rainy night, not so much!

And where is the way to the residence anyway?

I am frustrated! I want to say that this campus is grossly disorganized and incompetent, not at all customer-centric, and absolutely not user-friendly. That is my executive's mind working. I close my eyes and see myself at work, at the airport, in the cab . . . where everything has to work like clockwork or else! Sometimes, I still miss it.

Breathe!

Tuesday January 25

The campus is gorgeous. The walk from the residence to the classroom and back is through the forest, where dripping pine trees are so fragrant and the ocean in the background so inviting, that it makes it all irresistibly magical. Once you know the place, you don't mind that it is so backwards. You discover forgiveness.

Classes are great. There are thirty of us. Mostly women. A sizeable cohort made of people with outstanding professional backgrounds. As you would expect from a coaching class with thirty women, there is a lot of sharing, talking from the heart, hugging, and all. Not your typical classroom set up.

To top it all off, one of the faculty members believes there is nothing like getting up and dancing to wake up the crowds. Every time you come back from breaks, Bruce Springsteen or Green Day is on, and people are dancing. Takes some getting used to! But mostly, it is a lot of fun to be delinquent again!

About time!

Of course, the whole idea of coaching is to get out of your comfort zone! This will do it for me! I am mostly comfortable with all of it except that the introvert in me desperately needs some down time, and it is only Tuesday. It is 9 p.m. and I am returning to my room after a nice dinner with a colleague. I am thrilled at the thought of getting back to my room early, alone. I stop by the lounge to get a cup of tea and bump into a few more colleagues and a few bottles of Merlot! Before I know it, we are playing cards, and once it is too late to change my mind, I know I am heading toward a short night's sleep, and most likely, a remarkable headache tomorrow!

Oh, the life on campus . . . . What is there not to like?

Wednesday January 26

Other than being sleep-deprived and threatening to pack up and leave if I have to get up one more time to dance, everything is going well!

In fact, there is a lot here I am thoroughly enjoying. I feel somewhat like Asterix in the magic brew. (Sorry if you don't know the story; something about rebels in France before it was France and the Roman Empire.) I seem to have landed in a place where topics of discussion, interests, concerns, and readings, are all great, and better yet, I can share them with others who have similar interests. Sharing is the novelty. At work, the list of things we had to take care of and deal with was so exhaustive and pressing that, by the time we were done with the necessities of work, there was no time, no interest, and as a matter of fact, no one left to talk to about exciting topics. I was used to brewing a lot of these in my head.

I'm finding I do a lot of stuff in my head.

Maybe this habit of talking to myself is a good thing after all. Had I said out loud everything I said to myself over the course of my career, I may have ended up in jail instead of university. Who's to tell? Hard to know how people react sometimes.

Come the weekend, it is time to hit the road again. I am flying to Ottawa tomorrow, so I need to get home first to unpack, and then pack again!

Sunday January 30

Tem and I are invited for dinner tonight at our new friends' house. It is always exciting to walk into someone's life for the first time. I love stories, backgrounds, and how it all comes together. I am curious about the pictures, the glassware, the coats hanging in the hall, the books. They all have a story. I love people's stories.

I wonder how people would interpret my life if they walked into my condo today. How would they know all there is to know? The years in Europe, the trips to Asia, the summers at the lake, the heart breaks, the joy, the sleepless nights, the burnt toasts, the stains on the rugs? All these little things adding up to a life.

Maybe, just maybe, wanting people to know these things, which explain how your life adds up, is where the urge to write comes from. Wanting people to know, to understand, and to love my story, and wondering whether or not my outward self tells it like it is.

What do I care what people think of my life? Good question. I have thought about that a lot.

I like my life. I think it is a rich one, and as with everything else one loves, one hopes others will love it too. Maybe it is just that simple.

Or maybe my outward life does not show the real me from the inside, and now I want to show it, just like how the perpetrator of a crime left unpunished for many years can't stand it anymore and comes forward to confess? I know. This sounds crazy, but I am not. This is just my mind trying to understand itself.

At twenty, I thought that by the time I reached fifty-five, I would have children, probably four, perhaps grandchildren, a house, but no mortgage, a cottage where the children, my husband, and I would gather regularly. Summers would be on the golf course, and winters mostly on my skis, cross-country, I was thinking. Invariably, weekends would be for family gatherings where I would cook a big meal and have all my loved ones around the dinner table.

Turns out, reality did not quite match the dream.

Instead, I live three thousand miles away from my kids, no grandkids yet, and that's okay really; my mortgage will last me a lifetime, and last time I moved, I dumped all the dishes and furniture that were intended for the cottage-to-be. There isn't gonna be any cottage. Don't have time or money to play golf, have not put cross-country skis on in years (Why would I? I live an hour away from Whistler, Canada's finest ski resort and home of the 2010 Olympics), and I hate cooking.

So, it's not that I don't like my life, but it took me by surprise. I just did not see it coming; that's all.

Tuesday February 1

I am in Montreal. I always feel I need to specify, because after all, it is a highly volatile piece of data. I have a nine o'clock appointment today. Another former colleague with whom I was on a board previously. We are meeting at his office. He is well-established and hugely successful in the coaching arena in Montreal. I want to understand how coaching is alive and well in this city, who pulls the strings, who is heavy, how many independents there are, you know . . . all that stuff you need to know before entering a market.

I am trying to focus on what he says, but I am distracted by the luxury of the office around me. I am trying to listen to what the paintings on the wall, the smell of leather furniture, the choice of colors are telling me.

Can coaching be this lucrative?

In the end, I am more intrigued by the decor than the host. He is interesting all right, but mostly, he is telling me about his story, his experience, his view of the world. Often, I am beginning to find, there is the same feel to these stories. The feel is that of a long tunnel full of closed doors. Every door has a name on it, and it ain't mine. The room is taken. People like to describe their world as unique and inaccessible. Somehow, they make it look like they got in just in time because that which they have is no longer available. Somewhat like the limited time offers at your retail store or the low fare seats on Air Canada.

So, enough of that testing of others' lives to see whether they fit mine. I have decided that I will build my own as I go. There I go again, making it on my own, my own way. I don't seem to be able to get away from that pattern. No sense trying to get a piece of theirs. For the most part, they are not sharing.

No hard feelings. I get it. What we build is ours. Some people believe that it gets better by sharing it. Others think it gets safer by protecting it.

Our visit is friendly, interesting, and informative nevertheless.

Thursday February 3

I am back in Vancouver. I have four days to get ahead in next week's reading for university and also get ready for next week's Myers Briggs class. I am double dipping. I registered for a Myers Briggs certification program taking place here next week. Myers Briggs, in a nutshell, is the layman's tool to apply Carl Jung's theory of personality traits to the work place (or wherever you want to apply it.)

In my career, I have used Myers Briggs quite a bit while working with individuals and teams. It is a powerful tool to help you understand why the communication dynamics are the way they are. At least, we typically presented it that way. In reality, it is particularly helpful in figuring out what the heck makes Larry tick! Anyhow, I always wanted to get a more in-depth knowledge of the tool. Now I have time to do it. Class starts next week, and I have the weekend to catch up on my reading, of which there is a lot. So, I dive in.

I do not find time to eat, shower, get dressed, or even go down to pick up the mail. I love it. I don't want anything distracting me from what I am doing. The pace is great. At long last. I do what I want for as long as I want. To be perfectly honest, I am concerned that maybe, just maybe, I am on the verge of becoming impossible to live with (or is it too late already?). What would I do with a child, a 24/7 husband, or a job? I can hear this already: "Honey, we have to talk . . . ." Cringe . . . .

This over-the-top, outrageously self-centered, totally dedicated immersion in what I do is utterly delicious. It is what I consider my reward for having worked full-time, and raised three kids on my own with that brain of mine always begging for more time and attention. To make up for all the times where I had to split everything a hundred ways and barely participate in anything significantly because quantity always superseded quality, now I can indulge. I can see already that there is no telling when I will tire of that!

Friday February 5

To prepare for the workshops taking place next week, I complete the latest online profile assessment, which tells me, not surprisingly, that writing is a field of interest for me.

I can be slow on the intake sometimes, but I get it now.

Fifty-five years it took me to get here! It is a little embarrassing for me to admit it publicly, I mean the interest in writing, that is. Writing takes talent. Being talented in the business world is often a result of hard work. That I can do. Being talented in the literary world, for me, results from being gifted on top of producing hard work. This is how I see it.

How many people are comfortable to stand up and say they are gifted? I am not. Comfortable that is. As for gifted, I don't know. I have a hunch I am going to find out. So, put simply, some people need to run ten kilometers every day or others need to have dessert after every meal. Me? It is writing. To this day, writing is a luxurious, frivolous act. It is something I do after all "my work" is done. How can I turn the tables? How can writing become a priority? If I could make a living out of it, would it become a priority? Or should I look at this the other way around? If I made it a priority, then could I make it a living? And what if making a living at it was not the right measure? What if I redefined success to mean something else?

This is all kind of cool because I can make it anything I want it to be. Success is whatever I define it to be. Pretty powerful. Whether it is to look at a printed version of my book sitting on my coffee table and thinking "I did it," or it is making it on the bestseller list, success is whatever I want it to be. If I am smart, I will head for the book on the coffee table. I may be willing to be bold, but I have not gone stupid yet. I don't even know that anyone would want to publish this book, let alone buy it.

Still, to believe that writing can somehow contribute to support my financial needs is to believe that I can be the prima ballerina, the top golfer at the U.S. Open, or the gold medalist at the Olympics. It is to dream big.

What is the point of dreaming small, you might ask?

Good point.

Regardless of the outcome, I will do it. I will post, publish, sell, raffle, give away, stuff it in cereal boxes—somehow I will share my writing. It is my offering. Let's at least start with that and remember that it is not about how late I come into this process, but rather, how much time still remains ahead of me to get it done. Given my family genes, I'd say plenty!

Sunday February 6

I have this really weird habit: every so often when I am too tired to engage in any cerebral activity and need a break, I visit my bookshelves. My books are my friends. They are as visual to me as an open photo album on my coffee table. So, like friends, I visit them from time to time.

All my books have a date and the name of a city written in the front page. It is a wonderful daydreaming activity to go through rows of books and remember what space—geographical, mental, and emotional—I was in when I bought each one. When it comes to books, my memory is good. Perhaps it is because a book is visual. I need a picture to remember.

So, it goes this way; a pile to give away to the library, a pile to recycle, and a pile to keep preciously for my memoirs. In that last pile are multiple agendas from my working years. I leaf through the most recent ones from my last job. I read the daily tasks detailing what my days were filled with, and a sudden overwhelming wave of sadness comes over me.

Wow, another curve ball.

I try to capture the essence of it. It has nothing to do with regrets over the loss of that job. It comes from a place much deeper than that. It has everything to do with an incredible feeling of loneliness and of something not right by me. There was something I was carrying with me that may not have had anything to do with the particular job or the environment I was in. But then again, it may. I am not sure. The more I discover about myself in this sabbatical, the more I am stunned. My sense is that this sadness has to do with too much denial. Going on too long with too little and pretending it was all right. Of course, I did not know I was doing it, but deep down inside, something paid attention, and that feeling is coming up now that I have time to listen to it. Tom Peters said it right: If you are not confused, then you are not paying attention! I was not paying attention. Now I am confused.

So why did I stay in that place?

Well, for starters, down-to-earth considerations such as paying the mortgage, the kids' school tuition, and my retirement plan come into play. Then, one does not always know that one is in such places until she is out of it! A bit like not knowing you have spinach on your teeth until you come home at night and see yourself in the mirror. Thirdly, it was not all that bad, and finally, because I had a plan (see? I am not always so clueless), so I could be where I am today. Yes, I will admit it. I was one of those who went through months and years of her life saying, "If I can just get through this, then I'll be all right," and you know what? Unless you were born into loads of money and security, you have no choice, from time-to-time, but to go through such phases. It's okay. No different than training for the triathlon. Drooling, demanding, unforgiving, and relentless efforts are needed. In the end, crossing the finish line makes it all worthwhile.

You could say it had a happy ending, but considering that the ending is only the beginning, I am not sure what I should call it.

Tuesday February 8

I am in class again for four straight days. As much as I like learning, I sense some restlessness. A big chunk of me just wants to say: "Leave me alone." I am nearing the breaking point where I want to go out and apply what I am learning. I am not there yet, but it is coming—I can tell. All this team work, these group activities, this gathering of otherwise total strangers with whom I have to share my inner thoughts, preferences in life, behavior style etc. is hard. It just does not come naturally to me. By now, however, I have done so much of it that I am used to it. I do not fight it, do not resist it, and as expected, I benefit from it, but it will never be a natural inclination for me.

Wednesday February 9

Fascinating how life unfolds. I love watching it, particularly when it ties in with my theory that when you feel you are hanging by a thread and things are about to collapse, interesting stuff starts happening.

Of course, there is a reason why that is true. Once you have exhausted all actions and ideas and have no more energy or inclination to fight everything, you typically step back, and in doing so, you let life take over. More often than not, it is smarter than you—life that is.

In my executive coaching program, as part of our curriculum, we are to start coaching individuals as though they are our own clients. Because we are still students, and because, from time-to-time, our faculty will be on the call listening in for auditing purposes, this coaching is to take place on a pro bono status.

I initially have no idea where I will find these people to coach, but one thing leading to another, I have five candidates, willing, ready, and able! Friends of friends, people in my network. It is true what they say about networking. It is the best proven way to find your way to a job.

Also today, I find a coach for myself; it is also part of the curriculum. As with any other professionals, we need to walk our talks. When provided with the list of potential alumni coaches, I read the first bio and stop right there; an artist and a writer, left the corporate world to coach and re-enter the artistic world. This one is for me. I am sold.

A lot of this coach's pedigree brings me back to my thoughts after my daughter's "When did you stop being a hippie?" question. Besides, there is a lot of energy in this coach's bio, and something unconventional about her that is very inviting. I suspect that she and I will see eye-to-eye. I can't wait to get started.

Friday February 11

This afternoon, I am meeting with a "contact." Yet another one. He is actually the recruiter who headhunted me for my first job here in Vancouver years ago—a nice, friendly man. He is a coach in addition to being a recruiter. So I want him to tell me about "life as a coach." I am still learning and taking notes.

Whereas some years ago, I would have kept all my plans to myself (introvert, remember?) now I quite openly share them with him.

"I want to be an executive coach and only a coach. This is what I like. I want to do it alone, not as part of a firm, and I want to do it both in Montreal and Vancouver. On a scale of 1 to 10, tell me how lunatic or crazy that is, please!"

"Just a little crazy," he says.

Just a little? Wow. This is good. Just a little is good. I fully expected him to say it was entirely crazy!

"Because of the nature of coaching, you will not be able to do that only. You cannot fill your days with coaching alone. You will need to diversify."

"THAT is the crazy part?" Ka-pow! I can deal with that kind of crazy! I don't want to fill my days anyway! I want to use the rest of the time for writing.

La Di, Da, Di, Da . . . Life is looking good!

Saturday February 12

I have time to go online and create my business email address this morning. It has been on my "To Do" list for a while, and since I have some extra time because I was up so insanely early, I get around to it.

Just like that. I am always so surprised when things are simple. I truly, honestly expect them to be challenging. Perhaps that is why they are.

I want to use a Gmail account because I find that, of all the easy options out there, such as Yahoo and the likes of them, Gmail is the one that sounds the least silly next to a business name. So Gmail it is.

When it comes to selecting an email address, I quickly realize that every word in the dictionary has been used. I can only come near to selecting what I want by using word combinations. What makes it a little bit difficult is that I am still not clear on exactly what the business will be. Will it be consulting, coaching, or both? I need a name that can be used in French and English without difficulty. That limits the options significantly. I try all kinds of combinations, surf the web for inspiration, and in the end, my patience being notoriously limited, I figure that using my name is my best option. Let's face it; who else would use it?

Pretty safe strategy I am thinking.

Since I still have time on my hands and things are ticking along marvellously well for me this morning, I go to my LinkedIn page and decide to add my business address. I am quite proud actually to write my own business name on my page. However, I am not having any success despite the many attempts to include it. I contact the help desk, and the person there tells me that my business address is not a real business address.

The nerve! What do they know?

Turns out, a name is nothing without a domain. As you create your business, you need a domain if you want to be online. Not many businesses can survive without being online . . . even funeral homes are going social, and they have as captive a market as it gets! So, there you go! Gmail is a public domain and could not possibly be claimed as your business domain. You need a domain of your own so you can establish your unique location online where your website and email address will reside. Think of it as a street address. It is the cyberspace equivalent of the brick-and-mortar days of the local general store.

So I need a domain. Where the hell do you find a domain? Not a clue! It turns out to be quite easy actually. You don't buy a domain; you rent it. Not sure, though, who the guy behind the counter is. I know to some people this process is absolutely a no-brainer, but I am learning all of this as I go along. It may be interesting, but truly, I'd rather be learning something else. In any case, thanks to my strategy of using my own name, I am able to lock in my domain and email address.

I feel pretty good about that.

Things are coming off that list, baby!

Thursday February 17

Today is my birthday. I am in Montreal. I did not want to spend it away from my loved ones. It is still early, so I lie in bed, on top of the covers, enjoying the sun beaming in from the window. It is winter outside, and in Montreal, sunny means cold in February. It is warm and cozy inside. I feel lazy.

I am surprised at how tired I am still; seems like there is still so much to do, and it is all going so slowly. It is beginning to weigh on me. I just want to be done and be on my way. I want to know what the future will be. I actually miss the days when my agenda ordered me around. It was so much easier to blame everything and everyone else for overloading it. Now, I look around, and there is only me. Whatever is not right is my problem and mine alone. All this waiting and preparing and hoping it will work out are not sitting well with me.

At least not today.

I want to be in a place where everything is easy because familiar. Like hanging my coat on the same hanger for a while, or knowing where the coffee jar is all the time, and not wondering whether your neighbors are actually your neighbors or just visitors because you can't recognize them. The stuff that, unbeknownst to you, makes your daily life easy. Easy is what I am after here.

Right now, I want to be settled. I have this sudden urge to know what my life will be for the next eighteen months. I don't think eighteen months is so unreasonable after all.

So unlike me!

Whenever I start thinking of pulling out the old sewing machine or feeling the urge to dig through my old recipe books, I know that something in me needs a whole lot of attention. This is the adult version of a tantrum.

So what is it that is demanding such attention? Is my security threshold falling below its minimum? Is it anxiety around my interview for board directorship positions next week? Discomfort around the unemployed status? DUH! Does an athlete want a gold medal? A baby his bottle? Of course I am disturbed by all of this, but to the extent that it affects my mood?

Why am I not all organized by now?

Is my plan to be in both cities a crazy one after all? Is this too distracting? Why is it that, after all these months, I still feel the need to lock myself up and take the time to think it all out (again!) and plan it all once and for all? (again, again).

Is the notion of once-and-for-all a pure fantasy, or will I ever get there?

I go to bed with a headache, and I wake up with a headache, and yet I am under the covers for hours at a time, sometimes ten hours. In the days when I had family, kids, pets, and a crazy job, I still got up full of energy with half as many hours of rest.

Where is the leak?

I don't know. I don't let it slow me down completely though. I know one day I will get up and all this confusion and frustration will be gone. Sounds simplistic, but mostly, it's true. Things simply do not happen in ninety days. As much as I would like them to, they don't. Not for me, not for anybody else usually. I profoundly hate when you take two steps forward, one backward, and yet, that is how you move ahead. I am very reluctant to give up anything I have gained. But things take time. I know. I know.

Tem bought tickets to tonight's performance of the ballet *Gisele*. How appropriate, you might say, being that it is my birthday! It is by far my favorite ballet, and ballet is, bar none, my favorite form of art. So, this is a win!

The ballet is what inspired my name. All through her pregnancy, my mom had her mind set on another name for me. A few weeks before giving birth, sitting in the doctor's office leafing through magazines, she read a story where, much to her horror, the main character, a 1600 lbs. Holstein dairy cow, had my chosen name.

She changed her mind. A rare occurrence.

The following weekend, she was watching TV and the ballet *Gisele* was being presented. She fell in love with it and decided to call me by that name. I was born with a love for ballet. I kid you not.

I sit in row eighteen with a perfect view of the stage. The first act goes by in a flash. I brace myself for the second, the best. I spend the entire time holding my breath and wiping tears. Few things describe beauty to me more vividly than a prima ballerina. Tonight, she is masterful.

Monday February 21

Another Monday, another 8 a.m. flight back to Vancouver. This week I am starting my first coaching relationship. I am actually looking forward to it very much. I am glad finally to get to the real stuff, not just plans on paper. Besides, it will feel like I am back at work.

I am not nervous about it. I am not scared. I expect to enter the coaching arena the way a Labrador enters the water. Head first, fearlessly, and with much anticipation.

I pick up my mail and ride the elevator up to my floor. It is noon. I am starved. I pull something out of the freezer and zap it. A lamb and vegetable dish I made a while back. To think that all I would keep on hand was coffee and wine. I've come a long way already.

At first, I want to go for a run, but quickly, the jet lag catches up with me, the scheduled conference call is approaching, and I end up not going out.

Instead, I read, catch up with email, make a few calls—the usual day at the office as it has become for me.

By the time my conference call is over, and the follow-up work is done, it is 7:30 local, 10:30 in my body. I am cold, tired, and lonely.

The days tend to have a better ending in Montreal.

Tuesday February 22

I am meeting with the president of a recruiting firm who specializes in recruiting for boards. I am not too sure what to expect from this meeting, and I am not sure why I care so much about it either. All I know is that I have been preparing like crazy for it.

Walking to the train station, I am not even listening to music. I am focused. I am on a mission. I get there on time, relaxed and feeling good.

The building where her office is located is under construction. The business is on the second floor. There are no walls, no doors; wires hang from the ceiling, and jack hammers mute all other noise.

She quickly shakes my hand, apologizes for the place, and introduces me to her partner. He is the one I will be meeting.

I am thinking that I am off to a bad start.

It is too noisy in the office. We head out and walk up the street to a nearby café. He tells me they don't recruit for boards. They merely work with them in areas of governance. Their real intention is to see whether I would be interested in an HR position. My intention was to look into a board position. So much for that.

I am initially disappointed, but oddly feel relieved. The conversation is dynamic, lively, and interesting. I share my ambitions and half-defined goals at this stage as well as my concerns of perhaps not having a sufficient network to launch my business at this stage. We go back and forth. Obviously, he has nothing to offer, other than empathy and some advice, like joining a sports team, a running group, local business breakfast meetings, etc. The usual stuff about networking.

Seriously? Do I look like such a rookie?

One hour later, we shake hands and depart. By then, the adrenaline has withdrawn and things don't look so good. Why do I feel like a ten year old who has just been told she should have polished her shoes before going to the principal's office? Not sure.

Why did I feel so much pressure going into this interview? Not sure of that either. In my entire career, I only interviewed four times, and three were successful at the first attempt. The one that got away was the one I most wanted.

Something about not wanting it too much is probably better!

Sitting on the train, riding back to town, I am surprised by how very, very different it is to be the one sitting on the other side of a need; meaning, being on the outside instead of the inside.

It is hard. It is nobody's fault, and you can't get upset. You cannot complain either. I just need to suck it up and move on. Really.

I stroll down Robson, slowly making my way home. I get in my condo, drop everything, change into my jogging suit, not that I intend to go jogging, pour myself a glass of wine, and put my feet up.

I know it is only 4 p.m., but I am sure it is happy hour somewhere! I need a happy something.

I am calling Tem. I need team support.

Thursday February 24

This morning Jill calls. She is my new friend in Ottawa.

She and I are in a similar place in life. Sort of. She just walked away from a thirty-year career, a successful one at that, and I just left the corporate world, also a successful place. She could be of retirement age, but she still has way too much wind in her sail. I feel the same. She has a nice home she shares with her husband, and whether or not she works has nothing to do with being able to pay off the mortgage!

That is where our lives differ!

I listen to her telling me about her coaching ambitions and mission. Some of it sounds like my own stuff. She wants to help. She wants to give. She is targeting her own industry in which she worked most of her life because she would want everyone in it to do better, etc. Suddenly, I get a funny feeling. Are we looking to establish a business for ourselves here, or are we hoping to save the world? I am not sure we have the right angle. Is it Peter Drucker or Mother Teresa we have in mind? Is she right to want to stick to what she knows best? Am I wrong to think that may not be wise?

For crying out loud, will this ever stop? Not knowing, experimenting, testing, trying out, wondering . . . . It is all so exhausting. Am I in the wrong decade to be trying all of this, or am I looking for an excuse here? Why can't I be convinced and comfortable about it all? Actually, you know what? To hell with age, timing, and as a matter of fact, to hell with it all, including this need to plan and this coaching business! I am not planning. I am not anticipating, projecting, expecting, or any of that forward-thinking stuff.

I am going to sit here and write until my three books are finished, and if that does not work, I will sell my condo in Montreal. Living then will be cheap because I will have all that extra cash and I will enroll in piano, yoga, and painting classes, and work here and there on sporadic HR assignments when I get bored from sitting around. Better yet, I will sell both my condos, buy a nice place in the country with Tem, and write, paint, stretch, read, and curl up with the cat until the cows come home!

Enough already!

The only break I get from this merry-go-round is when I sleep. I know there is no value in thinking negatively, but let's be real here. Just because I know what the right mind-set is does not mean I have it all the time. I don't get to manage my entire life from the daily quote on my fridge magnet. It is a series of hurdles for sure; some higher than others. Some I think I can tackle; others I think, "Hell, no!" But what I am finding is that whether I think I can or whether I think I can't, I am right. I agree with Henry Ford on that one.

Friday February 25

Ouch. Feedback! One of our assignments this week from Royal Roads is to work with feedback: how to give, how to receive. After twenty years in human resources, you would think I have been around the block with this idea, and frankly, I feel I have.

But this is different. This is feedback from mature, professional, trained coaches, who have read the books, and done the exercises. Been there, done that. There is a whole lot of depth and truth around what they say. Besides the good stuff (which we always tend to overlook), they share with me that it would serve me well to connect my heart and my head.

There is that head again (aka brain).

At first, I think this means that how I am showing up in that team is as one heartless player, and it really bothers me because, honestly, I take my heart to these meetings. I like the team. But no, that is not what they mean. (I asked.) I take my heart to them, admittedly. I just don't let them get to mine that easily. My head gets in the way.

Interesting twist!

To be totally honest, it is not the first time I have heard that my head gets in the way. Guys told me that a few times before as I seem to recall! But seriously, to be facing that same reality again sends me into the thinking mode (how easily I go there), trying to understand how to do that, connecting my heart with my head, without letting the head lead. Then I remember what they said. "Don't think about how it feels; just feel it."

Are we talking guts here?

It is an interesting exercise. Like an internal X-ray of my emotional process. Stuff happens, and it goes straight to my head. Head rejects it and sends it back to heart. Heart is upset because it does not want to deal with it, so it tries to send it back to head.

You can tell I have watched a lot of hockey games.

Here is where feedback steps in. It stands in-between head and heart and imposes its ruling on the heart. Think of it as the referee. You can't argue. Once a ruling is forced upon it, then heart rises to the task, opens up, and embraces the feeling. It is sticky at times, but mostly very informative and liberating.

Man! Life was simple when all I had to do was fix breakfasts, tie shoelaces, and pack lunchboxes. There was no time for internal heart/head battles then.

It is only noon. I am exhausted, and I have friends coming over for dinner tonight. I am also getting ready for Julie to come home tomorrow for spring break.

The weather is uncharacteristically winter like today. It is snowing heavily, which is an anomaly for Vancouver. There will be no BBQ; that is for sure. Instead, I decide to make some comfort food and go for boeuf bourguignon.

I know the movie *Julie & Julia* made a big fuss over boeuf bourguignon, but frankly, for me, it has always been a household item. My mom frequently made it, which is probably why today, on a cold, wet snowy day, I feel like making it. Everyone enjoyed it.

The city is completely snowed under when my friends leave after dinner. It is even more so when I wake up at 4 a.m.

It is disappointing that Julie will be coming home to a cold, snowy city. On the other hand, it is spectacularly and delightfully quiet.

Tuesday March 1

I am coaching today—a pro bono client, but a client just the same. I can see how there is a bit of a twist to this new career compared to my former job. Over time, I had developed serious problem-solving skills. Anyone with a problem could come to me for a solution or a path to a solution.

Coaching brings about transformation in individuals who then bring the solutions. It is a lasting approach. It is not so much about answering the questions anymore as much as questioning the answers:

a re-positioning for sure. So, when I sit across the desk from a smart, efficient, up and coming young executive, who talks about three—and five-year plans and the need to increase the organization's capacity, I get all geared up and want to jump in and tell him what to do.

Holding myself back is particularly difficult because he would like nothing more than for me to give him the answer, assuming I have it.

But then that would be my answer. Not his. This is similar to giving a fish, versus teaching how to fish. You know the story. It is a learning experience, no doubt. The real value of coaching is to bring the other to understand that he has the answer. People are capable. They know. They just have not had time to search for it, or the confidence to find it in them. Sometimes, they have it all, but they just don't know how to deliver it. It is all part of learning, and it can all be learned. I love it.

The drive back is quick, and I have time to stop at home and have breakfast with Julie before heading out again. I drop her off downtown and continue on to my own coaching session.

The meeting goes well. My coach basically leaves me with the thought that my coaching business can easily—"easily", she says—include coaching, speaking, and writing, and that making it in both Montreal and Vancouver is totally possible!

I like her attitude!

Wednesday March 2

I have an early ferry to the island this morning. I am on my way to the campus to attend some classes.

As I get ready to leave, I remember Julie saying something about hurricane winds being forecasted. I check The Weather Channel and I am glad I did. It appears that the entire island of Vancouver is surrounded by major winds and bad weather. Long story short, all ferries are cancelled this morning. It is 5:30 a.m. I crawl back into bed with my earrings on, lipstick on my face, and a whole mug of coffee making its way down to my bladder.

It did not work.

I get up again, happy to have all this time freed up. Of course, my brain immediately steps in and fills that white space with everything it wants to do: prepare income tax filing, read coaching material, write, go to the gym to get a personalized training program, go shopping with my daughter. It is excited. Instead, I do something I never do. I calm down, curl up on the couch with a good book, and read it cover-to-cover. It is about masterful coaching.

I put the book down and look out. From my living room, you can see the north shore mountains over the Burrard Inlet. It is such a peaceful view. When I am home, I start most mornings gazing through the window, waking my mind up slowly, in sync with the sun sliding up the mountains' sides. How challenging it is to believe that being idle and taking time to think and reflect are actually beneficial and not a waste of time? It takes extraordinary circumstances such as today, when a whole day clears up entirely and unexpectedly for me, to do this comfortably. This restless behavior is so deeply ingrained. I want to continue undoing it. I suspect it is no small task. To distract me from all that thinking, I do something extraordinary. I take Julie shopping.

When we moved to Vancouver, we discovered lululemon, the athletic sportswear store. It was founded here in Kitsilano, and at the time, was only available in Vancouver. Now, I can walk into lululemon stores in Toronto, New York, even Florida. But what Vancouver has now that others don't have yet is a factory outlet.

Aah . . . the factory outlet! A field day for a mother and daughter—a sunny one at that. The sun roof is open, the radio is on, as we sing along to the Beatles tunes and make our way to the factory.

On the way back, we stop for sushi. To be a mom without being responsible for your children's immediate survival is what freedom is all about! Nothing beats that.

Friday March 4

Julie drops me off at the airport for my flight to Montreal. With the price of gas these days, it is a treat to drive to the airport when I know that the SkyTrain will take me there for $3.00. But a treat it is.

I mean to work on the flight, but instead, I eat, drink, and watch the movie! Pretty close to being merry, I would say.

Six months into my sabbatical, and I am only now feeling like I can take three hours on the flight to watch a movie instead of "getting ahead." How wired did I have to be to be still unwinding after six months? Scary thought. The most upsetting part is that I would have denied being wired. I would have said I was simply busy and eager to "do my job!"

This raises the question: "What else is out there that I don't see?" What other behaviors do I display that are potentially hiding something else? How long will I be digging? Should I still?

For now, all I see is Tem behind the doors at the arrival terminal. As always, he picks me up at the airport, and as always, we get home to pop the proverbial "bubbly," a tradition we have started for ourselves. I bet if Air Canada got a hold of this tradition of ours, it would make it a trendy commercial. "You never know where your flight will lead you." On second thought, that slogan may not be all that smart! Most people will want to know where the flight will take them.

Just a thought!

Saturday March 5

We are driving to Quebec City to attend a friend's wedding. The weather is bad. It is snowing, blowing, and occasionally raining. It is slippery with limited visibility. It is how we know Quebec City to be in the winter. Yuk!

I share some forty years of friendship with the groom. After sixteen years in a common law relationship and two grown kids, his wife and he have decided to tie the knot. They do not seem to be concerned that damaging statistics out there state that couples who have lived happily together for years, and decide to get married, run into serious problems, including divorce in the years that follow. How odd is that? Is it that you can go further when you are not looking at the finish line? I am wondering. Will taking it a day at a time fool you into lasting longer? Evidently, this concern is not on their minds. They feel secure, as we all do on our wedding day. Fascinating how every couple thinks they will be different. When you say, "I do," all you are really after is the ability to sink your eyes in the beloved's and be with him or her for the rest of your life. It is that simple, but it is not so simple!

Champagne, hors d'oeuvres, and happy chitchats. Before we know it, it is dark; the bride and groom are on their way, and we are heading to a friend's place for dinner.

This friend, Pierre, is the one I have known the longest. We were in grade nine when we first met. This long-lasting friendship is dear to me and I am proud of it. There is a lot to be said about people who nurture friendships. He married thirty-two years ago, and his wife has become a good friend as well. Over the years, of course, we all lived our separate lives and went through various scenarios, not the least of which was a serious illness with his wife recently. We like to think that we share our friends' pains, but I think it may be pretentious to think we do. They alone face them head on, and only they know the peaks and valleys of such crossroads.

All I know is how it affects their lives. Besides the physical demands on her body, and the tremendous efforts it took her to beat this disease, what I see now is a new connection between the two; a taller bridge over deeper waters. For us, who stand as witnesses to their lives, it is emotionally moving, and a warm place to be.

I suspect it is as with any transformation in life. Suddenly, when you feel the bottom falling out from under your feet, you don't know anything else but to backtrack to a place where you recognize the surroundings and feel safe. If you are in a relationship, that often means that you turn to each other. If you can't, it probably means the end of that relationship. In reality, true transformation knows no back-steps. It is all forward. You make it alone, or you make it together, but you have got to go through it, and what does not kill you makes you stronger. It sounds harsh, and it is, but at the same time, it is a new road you embark on because you have a new perspective. If you are lucky, you get to keep some of the pieces of your previous life, such as a partner in this case.

As part of their new lives, my friends now have two dogs added to the household: a giant Airedale and a miniature one. One sleeps on my lap while the other eats away at my dinner napkin from under the table while we, two-legged humans, share what is on top.

This feels like a family dinner on a cold winter night, and that is exactly what it is.

Monday March 7

I am meeting this recruiter for board directorship positions. Another one. Same quest but different city. He set the appointment at 8:30 on Monday morning. Of course, I was not going to tell him that I have not gotten up that early in months except to catch my flight home. So I show up on St. Denis street at 8:15. It is a cold morning. I am a bit early. I order a large cappuccino.

He comes in. A pleasant man. I could easily turn this into a pleasantly social morning, but as planned, I go over my quest for board directorship again. What does it take? Who calls the shots? Where are the needs? How does one get elected? In a nutshell, his answer leaves me as cold as the ones I got in Vancouver.

"It is very much whom you know, and the best way to get elected is to be on a board already," he informs me, as if that made sense. Perhaps I should consider volunteering on government or not-for-profit boards for a few years and then . . . .

I zoom out. I get nauseous.

Another litany of steps and hurdles. Another endless list of chores. Right there and then, I decide to give up on this quest. I would have liked it, had it added something positive to my life. Right now, it feels like another damn triathlon! There is no energy around this pursuit for me! I am done reaching for goals that do not inspire me.

Truly, I believe I would be a great addition to a board. I have twenty years in HR, ten as a business partner in a global environment where everything from strategic planning, to succession planning, to restructuring, to employee retention, and bottom line considerations, were daily topics! And haven't I heard that an effort is being made to increase the number of women on boards?

Well, here is a silver bullet for anyone who is interested: To have women on boards, women will need to be hired!

It is that simple. Over and out!

The rest of the conversation is very pleasant. The nearer I get to the bottom of my coffee cup, the more liberated I feel!

By noon, when I meet my sons for lunch, I am in the best of moods. These days, I feel like all three of us are in the same place in our lives. Pretty cool for a mother to be in the same place as her kids!

One is looking for work: his first real job. One is contemplating an improvement to his current job, and me, I'm trying to create my own.

Those who are sad at the thought of their children growing up and leaving home need to think again! It leads to one of the greatest relationships you can have! It is a totally safe, unconditional, and forgiving relationship . . . and as a bonus, you get to continue to be a mom when you feel like it, and today I am being a bit of a mom. It is hard to stop giving advice. They are grown up enough to tell me when I have said enough!

Because my own quest to create my job is challenging, and at times daunting, I am thinking that it must be equally difficult for them.

This feeling that as a parent I know best is very hard to shed. Somehow, I think that the twenty-five years I have up on them will always allow me to be smarter. So, when they come up with better ideas or better solutions, another paradigm shows up in my life and I have to face it. Seats are shifting. Soon, if not already, they will know better.

And that is quite a shift!

Wednesday March 9

I am meeting with my coach today. I am still toying with coaching, versus mentoring, versus consulting, versus whatever I am compelled to do. I struggle with listening instead of talking, with waiting instead of jumping in. I just get antsy.

"What would you like to address today?"

Well, there is world hunger, democracy in Egypt, to sell or not to sell my condo in Montreal, but really, deep down, there is always only one thing: What do I do with my writing? I want to put my blog out there so badly, but I don't know how to reconcile it with my career. Will it help? Will it be a hindrance? Should I use my own name? A pen name? Who will hire a coach who started a career without a plan? I can't believe I am still asking these questions!

The hard reality is that the blog or potential book has little to do with the business. The blog is about my transition from the corporate world to I-don't-know-what-yet, the fun I get from sharing my stories and associating appropriate pictures with them, and the hope I have of creating an interest in the reader. I am not seeking to convince anyone of anything. I am not selling a miracle solution or a five-step system to stardom. I am merely saying that real life is challenging for everyone. Everyone. And there are too many people out there pretending otherwise and making others feel like they are not as good as others. Although many would have you believe a silver bullet exists for most problems, I want to say that, with help and determination, you can pretty much face anything.

Every coach will tell you that the most significant contribution to his or her career has been writing a book. So I am excited about that. Most of them, though, will tell you that the self-help book is the type you should write. You know, the how-to-in-seven-steps-success kind of book. The closest I can come to justifying the association of my book to my business is that my book is the reader's way to get to know me. Truly. Nobody hires a coach he does not know or does not like. So, if someone doesn't like what he reads about me, he will not hire me, and that is fine because I have already determined that I am done working with people I have no time for.

So the blog passes the muster test. I am going ahead with it. It has a purpose, even though it may be a risky endeavour.

I feel relieved and very happy about that decision. I need an outlet for this popcorn-popper-heat, move-over-Charlie, hold-on-to-your-shorts-and-hold-your-breath kind of fireworks I feel I have inside of me, wanting to come out! It is so big, so loud, and for the longest time, I did not know I had it in me, and now that I do, I feel like a cold bottle of champagne seconds before the cork pops! Watch out!

I am thinking that writing will bring it out, whatever it is that is so big!

The benefits of writing are many, and not the least is that it is cathartic. There is a mysterious process happening by which something unknown in my head becomes known through the motion of my fingers on the keyboard. A transfer occurs between brain and hands that I do not foresee. It flows, and what comes out is fascinating, to me at least. Not all writing takes place that way; there are writers, like there are bean-counters, who know everything that is going to be said and done before it takes place because they have planned it all. Good for them. I am just not one of them.

Thursday March 10

Tonight is my irregular, dependable Wings night! We order our usual, except "No blue cheese dressings on the wings, please," Ed says. "It is Lent," he explains.

"Lent?" Zoom back to my youth and my Catholic upbringing. Forty days without chocolate and sometimes without dessert. Forty days when you would make a conscientious effort to be nice. When you thought you could redeem yourself from all the slammed doors, curses under your breath, and wishes of never, ever seeing your sister again, by refraining to put maple syrup on your pancakes!

I am sure they—the priests, nuns, my parents, etc.—explained Lent better than that, but that was my perception of it at the time.

So, no blue cheese on my wings because it is Lent? Whatever!

Friday March 11

I am making up for the 366th day I got last week when all ferries to Vancouver Island were cancelled when I stayed home and read a book. That was nice, but business did not get taken care of. So, I am back at it today. I drive to the terminal and am there on time to board the 11 a.m. ferry.

Once on board, I lock my car and move up to the inside deck. I love taking the ferry. There is a vacation feel and a sense of freedom while you are "away at sea." It is only a ninety-minute ride, but it feels like an escape. Before long, it is time to go back to the car.

It is expected of every travelers that she (or he) remember where she left her car.

I seriously don't know where mine is. I thought for sure I did, but evidently, I don't. I go up and down rows of cars on both sides of the deck. Nothing looks familiar. I am starting to panic because I can see that we are minutes away from docking. I am frantically pointing my electronic door opener in all directions, hoping to see headlights blinking at me, but no. Nothing.

I could kick myself. This is not a first.

Once in Montreal, I had to pay a cab driver $25.00 to take me around the airport parking lot after I had been dragging my suitcases for what seemed to be an eternity, in my high heels, in search of my car. It was worse then. A ship is, after all, a known entity, and unless someone threw my car overboard while I was not looking, it has got to be here somewhere. Airport parking lots are a lot less predictable. You can spend hours not knowing whether your car is still there. Trust me. You can.

Just as I am heading toward the parking attendant to confess my stupidity, I see it, tucked away between two mini-vans. I swear I will not let this happen to me again.

I make it just on time to my one o'clock meeting. Then I zoom out of there to make it just on time to my three o'clock meeting, and then zoom out again . . . just in time to miss the 5 p.m. ferry. So, I park and wait in line two hours for the next one.

I am tired. These have been productive but demanding meetings. I am thinking that, once on board the ship, a nice cool glass of Pinot Grigio, while sitting comfortably in the lounge looking at the island disappearing in the distance, is a perfect plan.

Right after boarding, I look around for the lounge. I ask the attendant whether she tends the tables or I need to help myself.

"Have you paid the cashier yet?" she asks.

I don't like her tone. How am I supposed to know that you must pay first and then get your food after? So, I have not, mostly because I have not bought anything yet, is what I want to say to her, but I refrain. As I so often do. I refrain and catch myself and instead reply nicely, "No, but I will, of course; first I am inquiring as to how things work."

"You can have any of these snacks or drinks."

I look around but can't see any alcoholic beverage. "I want a drink," I say rather directly.

"You can have Ginger Ale, Coke, Diet Coke . . . ."

"No. I want a real drink; some wine, red or white; I don't care," I say, now almost impatiently. Come on! This ferry only lasts ninety minutes. Take away this arguing and docking, I have sixty minutes left. Let's get with the program!

"We don't serve any alcoholic beverages on any of the ferries in BC," she says with pride and conviction.

We may be tree-huggers, and I may love that about BC, but man, oh man, can we be stiff when it comes to alcohol. What are we afraid of? That in the sixty minutes the lounge is open a crowd of wild and misbehaved teenagers will turn into violent and out-of-control offenders?

I walk out and sit in the interior deck. I am pouting.

Before long, it is time to go down to the decks below again. Land is nearing.

This time I have paid attention. Deck number two, zone four, under the clock, facing the front of the ship! Deck two, zone four, locate the clock, and there we are. No car. This is not my car. In fact, someone is already sitting in this "not my car" car. How can this be? How many deck number two, zone four, clocks are on a ship? How does everybody else do it?

Up and down the rows of cars again. I encourage myself by thinking that at least it is not the same crowd looking at me.

Turns out, and you may want to write this down, there are two deck two's. One on either side of the ship, and by the way, ferry boats turn around at sea, so the front becomes the back!

It does not take me quite as long this time, but I search long enough to have people smile at me and talk to each other when I walk past their cars a first, second, and third time.

Truth is, I am not sure this situation will not happen again. Something about paying attention to details has not totally registered with me yet.

Tuesday March 15

I have dinner with a former colleague tonight. He and I joined the same organization more than ten years ago. Despite our successful respective backgrounds, and each for our personal reasons, we chose to leave the big city at one point in our careers, and elected to work for a company in a somewhat remote, rural area of Quebec. That was where we met. The road leading to the office was a dirt road, and at night, driving back to the city, depending on the season, you either watched for moose or bears crossing.

That was how rural it was. No pink martinis there!

Tonight, however, we are in Vancouver, shooting the breeze. He is now a successful CEO, and I am a newly appointed executive coach. He works globally. I am not too sure where I work, but technically, I can work anywhere. Impulsively, I offer to coach one of his employees on a pro bono basis, since I am still looking for volunteers. He says he'll think about it.

They all say that. I drop him off at the airport and drive home.

Friday March 18

I have the weekend to get ready for next week. I will spend it with Tem in Whistler, a ski resort north of Vancouver. We planned this trip quite a while back and have been looking forward to it with great anticipation.

About planning and anticipation: If anyone looked at my agenda of the last ten years, they would see that I never booked a vacation or time off more than a few days in advance. I never wanted to decide in April what I would do in October. Never. The resistance to planning was to allow for more spontaneity, or so I always said.

The real reason I now believe was that you could not get me to commit to anything—not even a week in the Bahamas!

I have learned the magic of vacation planning with Tem. If we want to go anywhere together, we have to plan it several months ahead of time. That is how his calendar works. What I am finding out is that by planning ahead, for starters, I do get to go—already a significant improvement over my methodology that allowed me to go away on vacation only when my calendar was freed up. Good luck with that!

Then, by planning ahead, I also plan the impact on my workload better. This means I don't have to work 'til I drop before and after the vacation, or at least not as much.

And, I get to look forward to it. I remember reading about how the greatest benefit of a vacation is the anticipation of it. Well, I sure missed out on that one, year after year.

So, Tem will be here on Thursday, and we will be off to Whistler. In order for me to enjoy the week, I need to put a few things to bed before I leave: Synchronizing my calendar with my personal and business email when my business email is on a domain my BlackBerry server will not recognize, shopping for a new printer because the old one just died, completing my Facebook and Twitter accounts before I can print my business cards, and the reason why I have not completed these accounts is because I won't know what to do with them once I have them. Sorry. I am of that age group.

Thursday March 20

I pick up Tem at the airport just before lunch. I have not packed so we have to stop at home to pick up my gear. It is on the way anyway. We have a bite to eat and find ourselves lazy. Our plan to head out early, so putting in a few hours of snowshoeing is shot.

It is fine. We are on holidays. Who wants to go snowshoeing in Whistler anyway?

If you ever drive the Sea to Sky highway heading toward Squamish from Vancouver, driving past Horseshoe Bay, you will see how beautiful that road is. You are literally caught between the sea and the sky, and the only place to go is to the mountains. Since the 2010 Olympics, the roads have improved; they were spectacular and life-threatening; now they are only spectacular.

We settle into our room and head out to the village. I love Whistler. Unlike many other ski resorts, this one is very casual. You are who you are and nobody minds. It is a young crowd.

Turns out we have a week of spectacular skiing.

Tem is a very elegant man, and that is true on skis as well. The runs are so wide, and there are so few people that we ski side-by-side, waltzing our way down the glacier. A most pleasant time.

The snow, the sun, the weather, everything is perfect, and to top it all off, I sleep like a baby every night of the week. Sunday comes way too soon, and before we know it, Tem is on the plane heading east, and I am driving home, facing homework and assorted duties.

Sometimes, I let my mind wander, and I wonder whether my life would be this good all the time if I were to retire?

Thursday March 27

I have an all morning meeting with the executive forum group. In her discussion, the leader is very clear in her statement for membership. "If you decide to become a consultant, you cannot stay in this executive group." That would be me! I agree with this statement in principle, but nevertheless, it feels like getting the boot!

My last galleon of an executive's life is sailing away. It feels somewhat like having to take your wedding dress wrapped in blue tissue paper and give it away because you need the closet space. It no longer fits you, and you could not possibly wear it anywhere, so there is no reason to hold on to it, but you do. Same kind of silly thing.

It is uncomfortable and somewhat sad. Losing that status definitely feels like a step back.

Now what? It is me versus the thousands of coaches the world over who have had time to develop their market, their website, their marketing tools, their approach, their network, their niche, and me, not even knowing how to create my Twitter account!

David and Goliath flash before my eyes.

Friday March 28

The only time in my life when I enjoyed jogging was more than thirty-five years ago when I was a newlywed and lived on Vancouver Island for the summer; I went running with a group of people along the docks and loved it. Since then, every time I tried, bar none, I hated it. I tried enough times to develop a certainty that I would never be able to run and enjoy it.

After a week of intense skiing, and in consideration of my efforts to stay fit and slim (or rather get slim again), I thought I should try picking up running again.

So I have been running every day this week, trying to put in as many minutes of continuous effort as possible. I started with ten, then fifteen minutes, and today, I ran the whole thirty minutes almost effortlessly! I must admit, though, that having Stanley Park as the backdrop to your running makes it easier. Granted.

The point is, when I can run and not think that I am running, I can do it quite easily. Conversely, when I start running, thinking I have thirty minutes to put in, in no time I feel tired and want to stop.

What this contradiction tells me is the same thing I have been learning, reading, and hearing all my life. "It is not the destination that counts, but the journey." Make sure you focus on the right thing.

I am sure this phrase was on your fridge or your desk at one time in your life. Keep it there. It is true.

What is also true, but of a much lighter subject, even though equally mind-boggling, is that I am now on my eighth day of back-and-forth between my mobile phone provider, my Internet/phone provider, and my new domain provider, also referred to as Mobile, Internet, and Server, trying to connect them all.

I don't want to age myself here by saying, "In my day," but it is unbelievable how much I miss human beings, and how I wish there were still a few to talk to me when I dial a customer service number.

Remember how excited I was when I created my domain name? It was as simple as I was told. Took but a few minutes, and cost me only ten dollars.

That was all very well so long as I did not want to do anything with it.

To be able to access my domain from my Mobile, I need to buy the Plan Plus package (figures!). So I do. Then I purchase the upgrade in order to create my POP/IMAP account (don't know what a POP/IMAP account is? Suck it up; this is only the beginning!)

I call my home PC maintenance guy to ask for help, but he is not familiar with BlackBerry technology. He is "on the other side." That would be Mac! Seriously? Why did I contract him to start with then? Why am I finding this out now? Another question I did not know to ask!

I call the geek squad, willing to pay $125 to get this fixed, so sick am I of it all. The technician says there is no point in him coming over. It is a simple download I should be able to get from my Mobile provider. Nothing gets me more nervous than a technician telling me it is simple!

I call Mobile and am told I need to buy an application ($125) to access my company. I am starting to lose it. As a matter of fact, Bob, or is it Rob, at the other end of the phone, gets the piece I lose, I think. He did not see it coming. I offload all the built-up frustrations and then feel badly about it because I know it is not Rob's fault. Actually, it appears to be nobody's fault, but it sure is driving me crazy.

I don't need an application to connect with my company! *I am* the company. It is me! This is not IBM or NASA. There are no fire walls,

VPN, or other protocols. People! It is just another email account, for crying out loud.

The next guy agrees with me. I do not need to buy the application. There. Finally some sense in the midst of that spinning madness. However, he believes something is wrong with my phone, so he suggests I call the manufacturer.

I think someone just started the tape over again . . . . I should go back to the store where I bought it, and have someone look at it.

Not going there. You're on the wrong page, buddy. I am past this.

I actually connect with a technician and explain (again!) my problem.

"You need the assistance of our specialized technical team."

At this point, I need a stiff drink far more than I need a technician.

"I will transfer you to our sales department first."

"NO! Whatever you do, do not transfer me. What do I need to talk to the sales department for?"

"You need to register first for this type of service," he says. "First call is $50."

What!!??!?

I find some of what I lost with Rob and give it to him as well!

I can't do this anymore. Truly I can't. What are we doing to ourselves, people? I am downright exhausted.

I have accomplished the square root of nothing.

Saturday March 29

So it is Saturday. I know Mobile, Internet, and Server are all open today, but I am still raw from yesterday. I don't want to deal with it; besides, I have a former colleague in town for twenty-four hours, and today, I committed to showing him the city.

It is a sunny day. He does not know it, but he is lucky. Sunny and weekends don't always match in Vancouver.

We take the ferry across False Creek; it is a small creek with small boats. Think of them as mini-tugboats, like the ones floating next to the rubber ducky in your bathtub if you have young children. I am explaining to my friend the challenges I have had with Mobile,

Internet, and Server this week. The captain overhears me talking and asks, "Do you have BIS?"

"Excuse me?"

"Sorry. I did not mean to eavesdrop, but I heard you say you are having problems. Do you have BIS?"

"And BIS would be?" I ask.

"BlackBerry Internet Services," he replies.

"Of course I do! I have been receiving my email for over a year."

"Does not mean you have BIS."

I show him the phone. He plays with the keyboard single-handedly while he docks the boat. "You have no BIS," he says. "That is why you can't connect!"

WHAT? Hours on the phone with the "experts," and countless emails from Mobile and Server providers telling me what to do, and not one of them ever mentioned that!

"How would they know you don't have BIS?" my friend asks.

How would they know? How would they know? Are you kidding me? They know when I cross the border. They know the minute my long distance calls go over the limit. They know when I am trying to download data, and how much of it, the last book I bought, and the tunes I download from iTunes. I am not sure, but I think they know what time I go to bed, too. Are you telling me they would not know I don't have Internet when I am calling them on the hour, every hour, for days?

Okay. He is a friend. I don't need to wring his neck.

They know, but they do not think of checking. Nobody nowadays has a smartphone without Internet. They don't even ask. They just assume.

Beware of assumptions.

I, of course, foolishly thought that receiving email meant you had Internet, by default. So, of course, I never purchased BIS. I did not know I had to.

I surrender. I will add BIS to my services. I am thrilled already because now I will be able to access my domain via my BlackBerry.

To think THAT would be a source of happiness one day! Sometimes, I am afraid I have been cast in *The Incredible Shrinking Life*!

Monday March 31

Once there was a guy called Mobile, another called Internet, and a third named Server . . . . If you are sick of hearing about them, just think of how I feel dealing with them. This is now a saga of great proportion, and I am finding it so greatly therapeutic to write it all down, so bear with me.

I call Mobile. I want to purchase BIS. It should be easy because I know all the humans are in the sales department. You need to ask them all your questions before you pay, though. Once they have your credit card number, they turn into tapes!

I have BIS now, and it still does not work. Somehow, I am not surprised.

Julie would say it is because I am not thinking positively about this situation. The mother I am would smile and say nothing, but the customer I am would say, "Honey, if I am capable of thinking positively about this, then the human brain is truly an extraordinary thing."

I have run out of options with Mobile, so I call Internet. Definitely not an Internet connection issue, the assistant says. What a surprise! He suggests something is wrong with my phone.

Another one.

I'll tell you what is wrong. This whole mind-blowing, blood-curling, head-spinning outer space saga is wrong! Give me the techie again or put a fork through me! I have had it!

By the time I get connected to a real human being again, after endless meanders of automated services, he says he can't help. He does not think anything is wrong with the connection. He is trying to ship me off to some other department, but I won't let him. I don't care. I don't want to hang up. This is a real person with whom I can talk, reason, and ask questions. I don't want to let go of him. Please don't go! I try everything. I make jokes. I ask him what his favorite song is, whether he has kids. I even tell him I am writing a book, and if he can find the solution to my dilemma, he will be the hero . . . .

No sense of humor, that guy!

He can't help. So he says, "Please stay on the line and I will transfer you!"

NOOO!

Dead tone . . . .

The transfer did not work. For crying out loud! Didn't anybody pass the transfer 101 training in this company?

By the time I dial again, since the company is on the East Coast and there is a three-hour difference, their day is over and they have gone home.

That's it.

The things we do to ourselves! Who will my children talk to when they are my age? I sure hope their virtual relationships will work better than mine; otherwise, this is going to be one heck of a lonely planet!

Tuesday, April 1

Success or progress is sometimes measured in odd ways.

Ten years ago, I woke up with a lump on my breast. I swear it was not there the night before.

It was hard and painful, so I went to the doctor's office. "Unusual shape . . . a size that concerns me . . . ." The doctor had all kinds of encouraging words for me. He recommended a biopsy. It would take ten days to get the results.

What to do with myself? Ten days is a long time when you are scared.

I borrowed a friend's cottage in the Eastern Townships, asked Mom and Dad to sit the children, and I booked a week off from work. By myself. I packed my walking shoes, books, and paper to write on. I needed time alone with myself to get to the bottom of something.

If the biopsy turned out to be worrisome, it would mean facing the fight of my life. The fight *for* my life actually.

Was I up for it?

That was what I had gone there to find out. Face-to-face with myself. Ask a straight question and get an honest answer. Could I? Would I pick up this fight? I had to know the answer before going back and facing the verdict.

It took the whole week to come up with the answer, and it was the wrong one.

I was not depressed. I wanted to be there for my children. I simply did not have the energy to face this fight. Besides, what would I fight for? So I could continue to work around the clock, go through endless

"To Do" lists, and wake up as tired as when I went to bed the night before, to start all over again?

That is what was wrong. I decided that, should I be so lucky as to get a clean bill of health, I would never let myself be in that situation again.

And I did get a clean bill of health, and I did follow through with my promise. That is what led me to that time in my life when I tossed everything up in the air, but the kids. It served me well.

Today, years later, I am on my way to the doctor's office; another doctor, another city, another issue, but similar concerns. Technology being what it is, results are in much faster now, so I don't have to take a vacation to decide how to deal with it.

I had just enough time to check quickly on my readiness level to pick up that fight, should I need to. This time it is a resounding Yes! It is easy. Saying that makes me realize how far I have come. Why on earth would I not want to stick around for the good time?

My life at this point is like once the children are fed, bathed, stories have been read, and lunches are made for the next day, you sit down, put your feet up, and pick up that book. Granted, the phone will ring, or one child will wake up with an earache or a bad dream, but overall, things will have quieted down. Who would want to skip that?

Then it dawns on me.

Maybe this is a measure of success. This time around, there is no ambiguity, and lucky for me, I make it past "GO" again.

Wednesday April 2

I am desperate for a solution to my Mobile, Internet, and Server issue. It is still unresolved. I call my friend's husband in Cincinnati. He is a techie. I don't know where else to turn. He insists it is a server issue. I need to talk to the domain administrator.

These are the folks with whom I "raise a ticket." I think it is their strategy to avoid having clients talk to them. You send your issues via email; they fill out a form, and send an email to acknowledge they have received it. This is typically the only time you hear from them. They answered all of my emails saying they would get back to me within four hours. That was last week.

I bypass their system and reach the sales department. Remember, that is where humans hide.

I must be very dramatic on the call because the lady on the phone feels sorry for me and transfers me to Siva.

"Siva," I say, "whatever you do, don't transfer me, and don't hang up. PLEASE, hear me out."

I proceed to tell him my story. He listens. In fact, he even seems to care. I feel like fainting. This is so extraordinary. A novelty! He suggests I try again while he is on the line. I sense he wants to help. I feel compassion and empathy coming from him. I am in tears. Then I hear it: "Oh!" he says. "I think I see what the problem is. Do you mind trying again? I see there is a conflict. I can fix this."

Do I mind? *Do I mind?* Are you kidding? My hands are shaking as I type in the information.

He can fix this, he said . . . . He can fix this?

And he does.

"If you were here, I would kiss you," I say. "And I know it is still early afternoon, but I don't care. I am having a drink immediately after I hang up."

He laughs.

We have human interaction. He makes my day, and perhaps, I add some sunshine to his as well.

Imagine the concept. Human interaction!

I am so excited, so relieved, I feel lightheaded! I have more energy than I know what to do with now that this problem is solved. I am thinking I will go for a run. The song on my iPod plays, "Don't give up 'til the sun comes up!" How appropriate.

Thursday April 3

I don't know how to explain this, and it is hard to believe, but I actually look forward to my run now. The moment I enter that trail and start trotting, my brain takes off, and I feel great! I am now at thirty-six minutes. I must admit, though, that the last three minutes are hard to sustain.

You may think, "What are a mere three minutes?" Well, when they come at the end of thirty-three minutes of running, they are very significant, and they are definitely an accomplishment.

As accomplishments go, I am completing the mid-point mark of my executive coaching program this weekend. I have mixed feelings about it.

For sure, I am happy. One thing I undoubtedly got out of this program was the certainty that I want to do coaching for a living. I mean literally. I hope to draw a sufficient income from it, but the actual coaching of individuals, within a trusted partnership, to help others see beyond themselves and be able to stretch, is what I want in my life, as professional activities go. All the better if money comes with it.

I do struggle, however, with the environment I am in at the moment. An awful lot of my cohort seems to be having epiphanies on a regular basis, as I can tell. I am not comfortable around all that demonstrative endorsement of all we say and do. I am of the opinion that just showing up in the morning does not automatically make me beautiful, awesome, and worthy of multiple "wows" in a single conversation.

To me, that is over the top.

Sometimes, I think my introspective stage is behind me now. Enough. Although I recognize one can always do more, for now, I am in the mood for a break. Been there, done that; now let me go! And so I spend the weekend completing what the faculty calls the "foundation document." It is intended to describe, in no uncertain terms, my vision and mission in life, why I am who I am, and by the way, whom I want to be for the rest of my life, in four pages.

Here is that box again.

I say that as if it were a useless exercise, but on the contrary. It is big, and it is a bone!

A real one.

For starters: I must define whom my client is. Well, fundamentally, what I have been exposed to in the workplace is the forty-plus-year-old male in a leadership position, a senior one, dealing with impossible deadlines, high pressure demands, and facing tremendous challenges with everything he's got in his life. It is costing him time, health, and maybe his marriage. He carries a significant ego, loves football, has no time for HR, and wishes everybody was as smart as him. He throws everything he's got at his attempt to be successful, and sometimes, even that is not enough. The more he works at delivering results, the more he alienates his team . . . sort of. Or the more he succeeds at taming dragons, the more dragons come his way. He is squeezed from all sides.

This is one size fits all. Applies to women just the same.

So, I say, "He," but that is only because that is mostly what I have known. We women are totally capable of being as messy and as messed up as any guy!

Then: What am I? A coach is a partner. One who is standing outside the fire with the watering can in her hands. She has had a full night's sleep and time to eat breakfast. She can think straight and see the forest because her face is not against the tree.

She is a great help. She saves you time and effort, and mostly, walks by you as you find your way to bigger and better things.

Coaching delivers extraordinary results. It is true. I have seen it.

People are skeptical, so they often question coaching. I can't blame them, but really, it is easy. Think of a time when you were able to partner with someone who had knowledge, experience, time, and truly cared about your success. You had her undivided attention. How did that work for you?

How many people in your life have no agenda when it comes to you?

So, I feel I can associate with both men and women equally. Ideally, in this day and age, they are one and the same. A woman is, hopefully, no longer a rare sight in the boardroom, and a forty-year-old male, I sure hope, has parental duties adding stress to his schedule. What can I say? I was brought up to share everything.

In both instances, it is lonely, exhausting, and difficult to sustain, yet rewarding, exciting, and addictive.

So, my foundation document needs to define whom my customers are and what I have to offer, among other things.

I need to find a way to position myself, not as someone trying to give directions; nobody wants to admit he is lost, but as someone helping you find a quicker way. Everybody loves a tip!

Coaching is for winners. To make them go deeper and faster.

It rocks!

Tuesday April 8

My coach works with me, helping me find my way through the meanders of what it is I want to do. At this stage, it is more about how I want to do it actually.

The vision and mission conversation carries on. What I want to do and why. I want to give, and I want to connect. Fundamentally, that is what it is all about. I need to do it in a way that will allow my artistic self to come out, and that is mostly in my communication. I want to work with individuals who want to learn, grow, and test the envelope, and I want to be fairly compensated for what I bring to the table. I did side with Peter Drucker after all.

I am sick and tired of people asking me to define, c-l-e-a-r-l-y, what it is I want.

What is it I need to explain further? What is it that people don't get?

I want to coach leaders, develop meaningful relationships, bring a significant contribution to the world around me, work in Vancouver, Montreal, the States, and the world for that matter. I want to have time to write because, truly, it is my first passion, and I want to get on the road as a well-known and appreciated speaker. I want to connect and reconnect people. I don't want to retire. I want to coach my way into the sunset . . . .

Why do I think I can do this? To start, I worked for more than twenty years in human resources, mostly in a leadership role, in countries around the world. People are my cup of tea. I see them. I hear them. I get them, and I can call a cat, a cat, every time. No fancy foot-stepping from me.

I can deliver it between the eyes just as well as the next guy, if needed! However, I know it takes compassion and care to look someone in the eye and say, "No, not good enough; you can do much better," and not get punched in the face in return.

But, to capture and summarize all of this in a few lines, on the web or otherwise, knowing that people will spend no more than ten seconds reading it, is daunting. Besides, if ten seconds is all they are willing to spend reading what I have to say, I am not sure I want to talk to them.

Here is a bit of an attitude maybe.

I get so carried away that, by the time I leave the tea house where my meeting was taking place, my patience not unlike the parking meter, has expired.

Wednesday April 9

The former colleague I had dinner with a few months ago, the one who worked with me where bears and moose shared the road at night, sent me an email this morning, out of the blue. Now he would like me to coach one of his key employees who is struggling with some transformational necessities.

Since I had not heard from him, I assumed he was not interested, so I went ahead and booked my time. He strikes back now with a desire to engage in a coaching program for one of his employees. He tells me of his needs, and I tell him how they can be taken care of. However, what he needs is too much work to be offered on a pro bono basis as I had initially done. Dilemma!

I offer to do the discovery part, or the introduction part, for free, and I let him know that a good job would require an additional four to five months, and here is the cost.

Had he been able to see me when I explained the scope and cost, he would have seen me close my eyes, tuck my head deep into my shoulders, and cringe.

Something is unbelievably uncomfortable in charging for your work when you have been a salaried employee all your life. It is a struggle at first, and one I know a lot of people have to deal with.

He agrees with the plan, and the cost, and he proposes that we meet next week to finalize it all. We sign off.

Wait a minute. Did I just contract my first paying client?

It is only April. I had not planned on earning any income before September at best. Now I am caught without a proper business registration, no business bank account, an unfinished logo, and an unresolved domain server connection!

But I am one happy coach!

You think your first client will be the result of a perfectly orchestrated business development plan where all the necessary tools and accessories are in place and in perfect order. Similar to how, as a young girl, you dream that your first kiss will be by candlelight with soft background music after your boyfriend says you are the apple of his eye. Instead, he kisses you in the backseat of a car while his friends in the front seat are listening to the hockey game on the radio!

Not nearly as romantic as you would have wanted, but nevertheless, still exciting!

Friday April 11

Philippe, my youngest son, is on vacation in Vancouver for the week. I suspect him of being in love with a girl here in town. With that in mind, he is looking at his work situation; should he elect to hang his hat here for a while? Given his field of expertise and his talent (this is the chef), he has a selection of offers to pick from. He is thinking of giving this city, this girl, this life, a try. As he does so, the plan is to stay with Mom during the trial period. He did not specify whether the trial was with the job or the girl.

Julie's school year has ended, and she is coming home for the summer: a combination of being homesick and having better job opportunities in Vancouver because of her network being bigger here. This is the daughter who had me put her life in boxes and recycling bins less than a year ago . . . .

"Well, honey, you will have to work out the sleeping arrangement with your sister," I suggest to him. "She will be here for the summer, and I am not prepared to have one of you camping on the living room couch night after night. There is only one spare bedroom, and it used to be hers, you know."

This is how, all of a sudden, my off-season clothes are back in boxes under my bed. My car is constantly on empty, and so is my fridge. The phone rings at midnight, and depending on who spends the night at my place (between Julie and Philippe), there may be an increased inflow or outflow of bodies in my apartment.

Suddenly, my space is no longer mine.

Some noise coming from the hallway wakes me up at 2 a.m. I get up to find my daughter all wrapped up in towels from head-to-toe. She just stepped out of the shower.

"Did you leave the water running?" I ask.

"No, Jim is in the shower." Jim would be the boyfriend.

"I see; then, who is in your room?"

"Louisa. She came in to shower and change. Do you mind if she sleeps on the couch?"

"Where will your brother sleep then?"

"At Jim's place. He will be back early for breakfast tomorrow. He needs to borrow the car; is that okay?"

Sigh.

She can tell that I am struggling with this level of activity at two in the morning. "Don't worry," she says tongue-in-cheek. "The aliens on the balcony have been told to be quiet!"

We laugh. Honestly, though, it is hard to see them leave, but anyone who tells you it is easy to see them come back does not have a life, or is lying!

I am leaving for the States tomorrow. I want a good night's sleep. I am meeting a new client, another one who came to me through a referral. It makes me wonder whether all that work around the website, logos, business cards, and all that visibility game online is not just a waste. In the end, I bet all my clients will come this way.

Leaving on Wednesday, I will be back late on Friday night.

Wednesday April 16

Going through the motions of calling the cab, getting a ride to the airport, checking in on the Chicago flight is actually nice. I hit the duty-free shop like a girl on payroll. Who would have thought I would ever miss greasy muffins and cold coffee for breakfast?? In Chicago, we land at terminal B, and I make my way to The Tapenade, only to find out that it no longer serves my favorite salad.

I've only been off the circuit for a few months . . . . Nothing stays the same anymore!

The second leg is a short flight to my final destination. Once there, I pick up my bag and my rental car and drive the ninety minutes to my destination. It is nearly 10 p.m. when I get there. All restaurants are closed. I am looking for a grocery store anyway. I want something light and fresh to eat, like fruits or a crispy salad.

I find such a store. Someone actually greets me at the door when I come in. The store is the size of JFK terminal with maybe five customers inside. It is 10 p.m. at night, and someone greets me at the door! They are open twenty-four hours a day! Why? Beats me!

The cashier is slower than the elevator in an old folks home, and people pay by check at the cash register. Where have I landed?

Welcome to rural America.

Incidentally, people here work overtime and bank their hours, so they can go mushroom hunting!

I am serious.

Where I come from, people go moose hunting or bear hunting. They carry guns, spend hours in a cache, freeze their butts, and stain their trucks with blood.

Here, they carry paper bags, wear sunglasses and sunhats, and make frittatas!

My kind of hunting.

Thursday April 17

My roller bag in tow, I show up at the reception desk feeling like a million bucks.

I never thought I would be that excited to report to work—to think that I would miss that!

In coaching, as in many things in life, the more you understand the "backdrop," or what made this place, person, or situation what it is, the easier it will be to define what it can become.

Life never starts here and now. It is a series of incremental events leading to a place that looks different every day you stop to look at it.

Today, day one, it is all about my client. Getting to know him: Where is he from? What does he do? What does he like? Dislike? Hobbies? Family? Last vacation? Previous jobs? Favorite book? And on, and on. It is an easy day filled with rich information.

I retire early enough to hit the gym again, complete some of my university homework, and make it to the restaurant for dinner before the sun sets.

In this restaurant, you can have an "all-you-can-eat" salad bar for $5.99. You have got to love rural America.

Friday April 18

Second session of coaching with my client. Today, we want to look at objectives. Ideally, employers hire coaches to support talented leaders in major undertakings. Sometimes, they turn to coaches to help equally talented leaders make it over a hump they just seem to be stuck on, and other times, they hire them because they, themselves, don't know how to deal with a situation. From a coach's perspective, this latter scenario is the most slippery.

A coach is not a replacement for a failed manager.

The session starts as smoothly as yesterday. We cruise along. All is well until we uncover a bone. We landed square on a blind spot, and suddenly, without being prepared, the blinders are pulled off. More like ripped off actually.

Oops! Did not see that one coming!

He freezes, stands up, and storms out of the room, not without slamming the door on his way out. I am left hanging, not knowing what to expect.

How is that for a first day on the job?

I am not sure what to think, or to do. Is he gone for the day? Will he return? How shall I face him? Should we change topics? Dig in some more?

I wait a good ten minutes. He finally returns. Upset would be putting it mildly. He comes back disengaged and totally void of energy. He alludes to the possibility of discontinuing everything.

"You mean the coaching program?"

"No. I mean the job!"

I swallow. "I see."

I am glad I am not reporting progress to the employer just yet because, at this stage, this situation may not be seen as such. Somehow, though, I think it is progress.

We part on good terms. I confirm our next meeting, and I let him know I will send him a confirmation. As I leave his office, I turn around to say goodbye. He looks like a truck just hit him.

Later, on the phone with my daughter, she asks, "How was your day at work, Mom?"

"Hmm . . . not too sure, honey," I answer.

I spend the whole drive back to the airport reflecting on this last session. It is a nice, warm, sunny day. The drive is pleasant. Endless fields of soft yellow grains swaying under the wind. Occasionally, a few cows spot the fields. I don't even turn the radio on. Nothing else is going on. I need to think. Did I do anything wrong? Was it me?

Silence creeps into my head, and so does comfort. This is what coaching is about. Whatever he saw today was definitely a first encounter. Until now, he never saw it. Sometimes, timing is everything; sometimes a simple word, a silence, a simple question will trigger the biggest reaction. You just don't know. What matters is that the layers be peeled off so the real issues make it to the surface. Once they do, in the vast majority of cases, they are fairly easy to deal with.

It is what you don't know that shoots you down. Not what you tackle.

All in all, I think it was a successful day—just not a comfortable one; that's all.

I make it on time to the airport and go through the drill of checking-in mindlessly. As the plane taxis to take off, it stops just short of the runway. The engines are shutting down.

This can't be good.

What now? It is not snowing; it is not raining; there is no thunderstorm, and I don't think terrorists have found where this airport is on the map yet, so what is the deal?

Turns out Chicago O'Hare airspace, where we are heading, is closed due to President Obama flying in the area. Imagine that! Have we gone mad? In medieval times, when the king needed to travel through the country, his aides would travel ahead to have the peasants and their sheep, cows, and assorted livestock removed from the road, so when the king arrived, he would not be slowed down.

Does not feel like we've made much progress to me!

We finally take off. I still make it on time for my connection in Chicago. A pleasant, uneventful flight, at least until fifty minutes before landing.

"Ladies and gentlemen, this is the captain. We have a situation we need to apprise you of . . . ."

This can't be good either. What happened to sit back, relax, and enjoy the flight?

Of all the flying hours I have logged in my life, this is the first time I hear such a message. He is saying that we may have to consider a belly landing. Not to worry; if we do, the fire trucks are all lined up waiting for us. I know this is intended to be a comforting statement, but somehow, it does not entirely have that effect.

They will try a few maneuvers, and if the landing gear does not perform as it should, meaning coming down from under, they will come back to instruct us on how we can best prepare for such a landing.

The plane goes instantly silent.

So, here is the thing. It is true what they say about your life flashing before your eyes. I immediately think about what I would leave undone. What regrets do I have?

Much to my delight, I really have none. Of course, I still want to do a million things, but nothing comes to mind about what I should have done and did not get around to. I know people usually say, "I want to go to Paris, or jump off an airplane before I die," but to me, that is irrelevant. Having been to Paris does not make contemplating death easier, at least not for me.

Thinking that I will leave a legacy does.

My thoughts, of course, go immediately to the people I love. Do they know that I love them? Was I clear with them? That is the check list I go through. Not so much what have I done or not done, but whom have I been.

In the end, the landing gear comes down, and that flight ends like all other uneventful ones.

But do you know what stuck in my mind? The one bit of unfinished business I found?

Writing my book.

Damn. Some things die hard!

Sunday May 8

Julie and I want to do the grind together for Mother's Day. If you live in Vancouver, you know what the grind is. If you don't, well, the name says it all. Doing the grind is climbing up a mountain, literally until you reach the top. It is a well-known activity around here. People train, time themselves, do it for team-building exercises, pride, etc.

Everyone has his reason. Us? It is to celebrate her return as well as Mother's Day.

It is raining cats and dogs, though, and by the time Julie gets home from work, it is too late anyway.

Instead, we elect to do something much easier. We head out to our neighborhood bar to watch the hockey playoffs. Our local team is playing. The bar is full and loud. We drink wine and eat quesadillas while the guy next to me is hitting on me like there is no tomorrow.

All in all, a nice night!

After the game, which we won, we walk down a quiet street parallel to Denman, and make it to my all-time favorite bar in Vancouver, overlooking English Bay, where we have dessert and tea.

Walking back home, arm-in-arm, I feel like a million bucks.

Being a mom is hot!

Then I am brutally reminded that I am indeed a mom, and Julie is the young one. She quickly changes, borrows the car keys, kisses me good night, and leaves the condo in a flash. "Don't wait up!" she says and locks the door behind her.

Somehow, I think being dropped off at the old folks home is going to feel just like that!

Tuesday May 10

I am three quarters of the way into my executive coaching program. We are still working on vision, mission, and business plans. Wasn't I there already two months ago?

Crap. Can't I just go for a run?

Right now, my inclination is to say that my mission is to deal with whatever lands in my lap. I will face it and deal with it to the best of my ability as I have always done with everything else in my life.

All that going out for a run does is delay the process.

The reason why I dislike this exercise of vision/mission so much at this stage is because the more I think about it, the more I realize that, in the back of my mind, I believe my business will grow organically, mostly by word-of-mouth. That being the case, what do I need to define the plan to grow it then, I would like to ask. My hope has been to stumble on to one or two clients who would be handed to me by friends, I would work with them, they would be pleased with my work, and as a good story goes, they would tell others, and my business will take off from there. Frankly, signs already suggest that this may be how it will unfold.

Therefore, all these questions—whom is my client, what is my niche, mission, vision, etc., and how do I target the clients in a very precise manner so I can go after them efficiently—just don't seem to have the urgency for me that others think they should have. Now, I may be dreaming in Technicolor, but that scenario of how things would unfold is my natural way of doing things. I am not so comfortable talking about it, though, because I am concerned it may not be taken seriously and may look like a Mickey Mouse plan to some.

We have grown so accustomed in the business world to thinking that organic is too slow and will never get you there, that even I, at this stage, feel uncomfortable with this approach. How can I promote my business and be taken seriously when starting out this way?

I am convinced that a business developed through word-of-mouth has sound, solid roots. It just takes longer to grow. I may not be very patient, but I am very reasonable. I am not looking to grow this business into a high-volume, high-yield business. I am hoping to make it a significant, nurturing, fulfilling business for myself. I also need it to cover my cost of living, which is not at all extravagant, and to give me some nice financial cushion. By cushion, I don't mean a villa on the Riviera; I mean being able to help my kids, should they need a hand or should I want to treat them, and to buy some niceties for myself. Nothing crazy. I have everything I need really. So what about the discomfort? It is mostly because in the business world, where, let's face it, most of my clients will come from, there is no such thing as a project without a plan. It doesn't exist. You don't make it past "GO" without a plan. My former business partner would say all the time that hope is not a strategy. I know. I agree. It is not like I am sitting here doing nothing, though. I just don't go at it the traditional way. That's all. I suspect many will think it is naïve and dangerous.

I am willing to bet that, for me at least, organic will work.

Besides, asking me to determine all of the outcomes before I enter the market is like asking me to run before I can walk. Sorry. Too bad, so sad; that is what I think, and the best I can do is declare: When my sabbatical is over, I want to launch my executive coaching business. I only need a few clients at a time, and I need them to be split between Montreal and Vancouver.

Here is another comment I get all the time: "In both cities, simultaneously? Why?" "Because," I have said many times, "I love Vancouver, but Montreal loves me. I don't want to leave here, but I also want to be there."

The very least you can say is that I am consistent.

I have two reasons for feeling passionate about coaching. First the individual, and then the community.

How we know and lead ourselves has everything to do with how we succeed at work and in life. I call that "self-mastery." Then, clearly, the way we relate to others is critical to our success as well.

Once people know who they are—what they are good at, and what they suck at—and are truly able to recognize both; once they understand their fundamental needs driven by their core values, and respect that, life becomes a whole lot better for a whole lot of people. To stop pretending to be whom you are not, finally to be whom you really are, is incredibly liberating and enabling. It is all very powerful stuff. Freedom and wellbeing reside in authenticity.

Likewise, efficiency, creativity and team synergy, all leading to innovation and growth, also reside in authenticity, facing reality head on, and calling a cat a cat. Life is too short to pretend otherwise, and too good when you are willing to embrace that honesty.

Success is not in what we control. Success is in what we are willing to explore and discover.

And in my practice, I want to help people find and experience their own success.

Hey? Did I just write down my mission?

Friday May 13

After all that arguing and preaching about the benefits of organic growth, I get cold feet, and even though I still want to pursue coaching, I also think I need to be prudent and be willing to consider alternative plans. I give in and agree to the need of having a web presence. If I am serious about running a business, I need to be visible. That is what everyone is saying.

I resist the urge to do it myself and hire help. The good news with professionals is also the bad news. They know their stuff so much more than you do that it is easy to talk past each other and not know it. Misunderstanding is as easy as overeating at a shrimp and lobster buffet. Ideally, unless you know c-l-e-a-r-l-y what you want, it is hard for professionals to understand you. Just a heads up. That's all.

Wednesday May 18

When it comes time to design my website, I know this process is definitely bigger than me. So I hire a designer.

I interview three. Everybody warned me about "designers." Make sure you have this guy under control, that you maintain rights to everything, that you agree on delivery dates, etc. Beware, be careful, double-check, and on and on. The list is endless and worrisome.

So, I meet all three: a well-organized, efficient, and reliable one who inspires me as much as the doorknob; a dynamic, creative, knowledgeable one who has no time for me until the end of the summer; and an artistic, colorful, passionate one who can meet my timeline. I go for artistic.

We meet in an overcrowded, noisy coffee shop. He comes in with his Mac, his dog, and his camera hanging around his neck. I have my briefcase, my notepad, and matching shoes and purse. I hesitate for a moment. *Are we a good match?* I wonder.

I am so nervous, and my hopes are so high, that it reminds me of when I consulted my first divorce lawyer. I had prepared for that meeting the way you prepare for a rehearsal when you know your parents are in the audience. I was so afraid he would not understand me. I was not looking for a fight, just for a fair and peaceful way out of my marriage. Indeed he did not understand me, and I ended up not hiring him—the divorce lawyer that is. A fight was not what I was looking for. I wanted to understand how you make peace with so much pain and anger in your heart.

A lawyer was not the right one to ask. So, somehow I feel as though the stakes are as high with a website designer, and my apprehensions are similar to the ones I had going into that lawyer's office.

So, talking to my designer, I don't know how to ask for what I want because the web is still largely unknown territory to me. On top of that, I do not know the language and what a website can do. All part of my discovery process.

I know, however, the essence of what I want to leave the visitor with, and that is all I need to convey to the designer. He can do the rest, and indeed, he totally gets what I am saying. At least, I feel he does.

It is an exhilarating moment for me to meet with someone who understands me that well.

I leave the meeting in such a state of excitement. At long last, I am going to establish my business online, and more importantly, publish my blog.

This is really big to me. It is the culmination of hours, days, and years of daydreaming.

Monday May 23

Constantly checking my email, hoping to hear from the designer, I feel like I'm six years old again and waiting for Santa. Finally, his email comes in.

I open it like you open a Tiffany's box, with great expectations of being surprised and totally charmed.

The bottom falls out. I do not like what I see. He did not get me.

The visuals are dark and gloomy. The words are not mine. The colors do not reflect me. The logo is meaningless in my eyes. I am shocked. How could he have so grossly misunderstood me? Did we not connect really well? Did I not spend two hours telling him about me, what I wanted to do, how I wanted to do it?

How else can I say this?

Because he sent it late last night, and it is now early morning, I am thinking he is a night owl, while I am Miss Rise-and-Shine. Therefore, the two of us shall not try to meet at this time of day!

So instead of calling him, I sit down, and painstakingly go through every element of the site. Identifying the likes, and dislikes, what works, what does not, how I see it working, etc. in hopes that it will help him understand me.

Whether he appreciated the thoroughness and the time I took to express myself clearly, I will never know, but I can only suspect he did not.

Later on that day, he finally replies. He agrees to modify the site. Within hours, he sends me a new version. Within hours! How can it take only a few hours to capture all the content and passion I am trying to convey to him? I am nervous.

In reviewing it, even though he is not standing in front of me, I can almost see him showing me the finger. Nothing short of that. This is the effect it has on me. It is nowhere near what I was expecting.

Then I call him. "What is going on?" I ask. He is evidently upset. I don't know how to say to him that I don't like what he has done, and moreover, I don't believe he likes it either. "It is neither me, nor you," I say. "This looks like something I could have done myself. I want talent. Your talent."

He agrees, but he wants his talent to be the way he sees it. In his mind, I really have little to do with all of this, other than liking it and writing the check that is.

We talk about whether we will be able to work together and whether we should. In the end, we agree to continue.

With hindsight, this proves to be a mistake.

By the end of the day, he sends me a prototype of my logo and colors (for branding remember) that are perfect. I absolutely love them. This is only the logo. Not the website though.

He says he will send me what he has done so far for the website, and we can meet again when he returns from vacation.

Because I am so happy with the work so far now that we have made peace, and because I sense he is one who easily can be on edge, I elect to lie low while he is away on vacation. Since the website, in my mind, is still at the draft level, I spend very little time looking at it. What is the point? He is away.

Besides, given what he did with the logo, I am so confident that the website will be great that I am already thrilled with it. Now we are back on track.

Life is good.

Thursday May 26

It is the executive forum's annual retreat this weekend. Retreat, to me, sounds like when I was a pre-teen and my mom and dad would go away for a weekend with some church members. This is a similar process, different venue.

In any case, there are supposed to be twelve of us, but we end up being six. What are we going to tell each other for a day and a half?

Turns out, it is nice. Friendly and intimate and a time to reflect on what it is we want to do with our lives (fascinating how everybody is so taken by this), how we want to do it, and by when.

I have so much discomfort around calling the shots ahead of time; it is so counterintuitive to my nature, but I have surrendered to the fact that even though I am willing to challenge this planning process, no one else is. No point arguing about it. In keeping with this chronic need to plan, we need to commit to three goals, with dates and milestones, before we leave.

I knew I would not escape that!

Actually, as much as I dislike the exercise, I do apply myself. Of course, I have goals. I just don't like to publish them—that way, I figure, I can always change my mind, and nobody will object. But I am a good sport. I stand up and declare my goals: Put my business online (meaning website and blog) by July 1, secure a minimum of three paying clients in the last quarter of 2011, and get this! Publish a book by December, 2012.

My colleagues think nothing of the website, figure I am being lazy on the number of targeted clients, and gasp when I mention the book.

This response confirms I should go for the book!

Monday May 30

Vacations are over for my web designer. He is back, and I want to meet with him. Now I have all kinds of questions for him—questions and suggestions, of course.

When I think we are meeting to discuss the website, he expects to meet to deliver the final package and get his check. If I thought we had a tense relationship prior to this meeting, we move into nuclear armament after that. He does not let me question any of his decisions, and quite frankly, tells me to go pound sand. In his words, I am impossible to work with.

I don't need to elaborate on what happens next, but let's just say a saga that will stretch for the better part of the summer begins. What I anticipated to be the climax of my whole launch ends up being a painful sore because my most exciting and cherished project is going sour. What should have been fun ends up being a burden.

If I were a Broadway producer launching my most exciting show, a similar situation would be that on opening night, when the curtain opens, there is no light on stage, or worse, the wrong set has been staged. Something along those lines.

However, as we like to say, life happens, and there is no amount of wishing it went right to make it right.

In the end, I have to settle for something that is not what I want. I don't know how to argue with him. I don't have the words and the technical knowledge to win that argument. He has no notion of customer satisfaction, nor an ability to listen. We just don't make a good mix.

Thursday June 9

It has been a whole year since we sold the division at my former job. Same time last year, I was starting my three-month countdown to employment termination. My sense of excitement and near liberation was so great; I remember the feeling as if it were yesterday.

Even though it was intended to be an end date, it was, in actual fact, yet another beginning. The beginning of the end of my employment, and all that my lifestyle as a jet-setter meant.

Standing at the beginning of something is always exciting because you can make it anything you want it to be. It is a blank page, and you can plan to color it as you go along.

When you do embark on that journey, though, all kinds of things happen; you find out that not all colors are available. The pencil needs sharpening. There is no pencil sharpener. The pens you wanted are on back order, or worse, out-of-stock. There may not be the paper grade you wanted for your drawing tablets. You find out that, in many instances, you can't erase any of the lines you have made . . . . You just have to adjust to all of this. So, your plans, as smart as they may have been, are sometimes defeated.

At this juncture, I am not anywhere near where I thought I would be, and I have deployed far more efforts than I thought would be needed.

Also, I have exhausted myself dealing with doubts and feelings of guilt around not having prepared myself well enough, not having gone into this transition with a smart and sound business plan, not having consulted the right advisors, not, not, not . . . .

Beating myself up for having done things wrong, or not having done the right things, comes too easily, I unpleasantly notice. I am not the only one whose mind is wired that way. It is a natural state for an awful lot of people. However, I have learned that it is not conducive to success. What you think is what you are. May as well get it right in your head.

Beware of your thoughts. They often speak louder than your words.

Friday June 17

Tem and I are leaving for two weeks in California as part of our summer vacation. The first week is in San Francisco, where he is attending a conference. Meanwhile, I will work, mostly write, in my hotel room, and visit the gym, the pool, and the local scenery. The following week is vacation. We will travel to the coast. This is why I say I live a charmed life.

As much as I enjoy it, I have a hard time believing it is real. I always feel as if happiness is temporary and will end soon. I blame it on the business. Maybe I even make the business harder than it needs to be just to make sure I feed my mental pattern. As long as the business is not launched, I have a bone to grind and a potential for misery!

I know I am going dark here, but I think there is some truth to that.

Working toward the readiness level is what I have been busy at most of my life. Ready for what? Anything you want: My next child, my next job, the new house, the board meeting, whatever is hanging out there. Admitting to having arrived somewhere changes a whole life-pattern.

Now, as far as the business is concerned, I sense I have reached the "GO" part. The "get ready, get set" parts have come and gone, and now all there is left is "GO." I keep standing on the edge, leaning forward, on the pretext that I need an even higher level of readiness, waiting for the perfect angle, the perfect time to jump in.

I am scared.

It is one thing to think about it, envision it, budget it, and put your bags by the door so you are ready when your ride arrives. It is another to hit the road. I am thinking that I will need to drive. There will be no ride, unless I take the car and drive it myself.

Why do I have to do everything?

Thursday June 23

Even though this is California, where sunshine and tasty Merlot are equally abundant, I continue to worry about my website, and my business to be. The majestic beauty of Yosemite Park, Big Sur, the Pacific Coast, in addition to the irresistible charm of Carmel, are not enough to make me forget the battle going on within me.

Shame on me.

Learning to let go is as important as learning to ride the wave. I should know this by now, but somewhere in the back of my mind is this determined hamster insisting that nothing can be enjoyed until such time as my business is well-launched and established.

And launching starts with the website, and the right visuals for my website. I know. I am stubborn. I am still at it.

The chosen picture for my website is actually a view of Big Sur, the spectacular West Coast line south of San Francisco. For reasons I don't really want to explain because they seem so trivial at this stage, a whole lot of the dispute with my designer was around the visual of my front page, more particularly my Big Sur picture. It did not look right to me, and he would not change it. He said it could not be modified.

I am thinking that perhaps I can take a new picture of the exact same place and reformat it to make it look the way I want it to look.

I am on this like a dog on a bone.

Tem and I spend an entire day chasing the coast line, stopping at every belvedere, holding our breaths at every turn of the road, thinking the next curve will be it, the way a gambler thinks the next card will make him rich! We climb rocks, go down trails, hang over cliffs, drive on dirt roads, and handle a few near-death encounters on the road to realize after hours of this crazy hunt that the picture I want must have been taken from the air.

I stop short of chartering a helicopter . . . and surrender. Maybe, just maybe, I will have to give that picture up and consider something else.

Defeated, tired, slowly making our way back to the hotel, we stop at this most incredible place, hooked against the mountainside, hanging over the rough surf, in the shade of huge cedar trees. We pluck ourselves in huge, comfortable armchairs, put our feet up on the ledge, sit square in the face of the sun slowly setting, and sip Mojitos until our taste buds are numb. An incredible sight and a delightful activity. Great combination! What is even more incredible is that this man is still with me after all I have put him through this past year of transition, namely my restless self. Suddenly, a picture seems trivial, and this sense of do-or-die with day one of launching a website feels equally silly.

What happens if day one drags into day two? Or if a picture is not all that you want it to be? Are people going home hungry? Will a child lose his mother? Will the sun not rise tomorrow?

How smart one becomes when one encounters exhaustion. Giving up the fight and allowing my plan to become something else is very liberating.

Monday June 27

In the spirit of liberation and getting going, I decide to launch my website, ready or not, perfect picture or not. Enough fiddling around with a bad picture and pretending something else needs fixing.

I can no longer wait for everything to be perfect and ready. Even though I feel I have not been successful at defining clearly who the reader is, even though I don't like the picture, and the blog is not all I want it to be, I press launch!

Voila!

I am now part of cyberspace, with my name, my picture, and much more about me out there than I ever thought I would be willing to share.

That very moment when you press "publish" and agree to share so much with so many is memorable. It is memorable mostly because of what happens once you have done so.

That is nothing. Nothing happens.

They say that the hard work in publishing a book is what happens after you have written it, and that writing is the easy part.

Well, I am finding out that is equally true for creating your website, your business, your presence etc. Once you are out there, you are actually nowhere, and quite invisible. Then the real work starts. It is a rude awakening because, quite frankly, you have exhausted yourself just getting there.

If it were not for my sister telling me about my typos, which I am grateful for, I would not hear from anybody, and potentially, nobody will know I am out there . . . .

Incidentally, here is another blow to my ego that I need to deal with. Reality is that nobody, or hardly anybody, is reading my blog.

Come to think of it, reinventing your life is a dangerous sport. No need, however, to get heavy equipment and sturdy self-protection gear. The bruises are all on the inside. The protection for that part needs to be built-in.

Not only do you expose yourself way beyond what you consider the outskirt of your comfort zone, but now you realize that you have to reach out to people and ask them to pay attention to you.

Next time you watch sports on TV, look for the guys jumping on their seats, waving flags at the camera, while showing their bellies and assorted body parts. It is a little bit of an indication of what you might have to do to make yourself visible on the web. Somehow, you feel as ridiculous as you think they look.

But at this point, you are into this project of promoting yourself up to your eyeballs. There is no turning back. You will do what it takes!

And it gets better! Not only do you need to try to catch everyone's attention, but you now need to beg: Please visit my site. Please tell me what you think of the content, the colors. What do you understand my offering to be? Whom do you see as my clients? Do you like the pictures? Please like me. Please be my friend.

It feels like auditioning in front of the whole wide world for a part nobody invited me to audition for!

Is it just me, or would someone else feel also slightly self-conscious here? This, to the introvert that I am, is similar to turning me inside out.

Now is when I am grateful I have collected more than a handful of friends along the way because my friends are the only ones I can reach out to in order to get through this uneasiness.

Thursday June 29

All this time that I have been attending university, taking courses online, and reading, I thought I was learning. Now that I have created a presence online, I can tell you that here is where the real learning occurs. It will probably not come as a surprise if I say that I am not one to read the instructions whenever I buy something new. Why bother? It is a lot more fun to learn as I go along, and a lot more suitable for my highly impatient self. Not always the simplest route, I will admit. So, going live online totally suits this style. Trials and tribulations are bountiful and true to the style. They create the best school out there, and there is no recess.

Having an online presence feels like riding the white waters in a kayak, water in my face, barely staying afloat, rocks speeding by with no shore in sight. Exhilarating and downright nerve-wracking it is. Everything coming at me is mostly all new stuff. It feels like drinking from a fire hose. The output is so much; unless I learn to control it, it will choke me.

Wednesday July 5

I may have given up on a few things, but not on the desire to do things right. So even though my website has been launched, I am still at it, trying to improve it. I know I need help to do so. Because of my web designer's attitude, I established in my mind that he intentionally made it impossible for me or anyone else to modify that site.

This, in my mind, was about control.

I came to the conclusion that only he can right the wrong, and since I am unable to let it go, I will have to reach out to him in one desperate move to get what I want. It takes me three days to muster the courage to do so. I finally ask.

He does not reply.

I am devastated.

When the time comes for the reunion with my cohort at the end of the program, I won't even have the pleasure of standing up in front of them and inviting them to my site, boasting about my accomplishments, and showing what I have done with pride, in a manner I have so many times anticipated. Wanting to celebrate is a legitimate need. Because I am somewhat embarrassed with the end product of my site, I am rather quiet about it.

What a missed opportunity.

Sunday July 17

I am heading back to the island, back on campus to complete my executive coaching program. Once again, and for the last time, my cohort will get together and conclude this course.

I am looking forward to seeing some friends. I am mostly eager to move on, though. Cut me loose! Let me go! I want to hit the road here.

So I walk into the class somewhat aloof, being already somewhere else in my head. I just want to be done. When I leave here in a few days, Tem will be waiting for me in Sooke—a beautiful coastline town here on the island. From there, we will kick off our summer vacations.

I fast-forward myself to the end of the week, and wish everyone else would as well.

But then, the nicety of being around people who have time for you, appreciate you, and include you in their sphere, works its magic on me. Suddenly, I want to spend more time with them, feeling taken by how wonderful it is to be among friends and feel this safe.

So we come to the end of the week. The morning of departure, I wake up early. I feel the tension of the last day. I pull the curtains open to find a deer and her fawn peacefully grazing in the backyard. I smile. This is a sign. Going forward, even though I leave this place and these friends, they will remain within reach. At least that is what I want to believe.

The class ends. In fact, the program ends. Pictures on the front lawn, promises to write, hurried hugs and kisses, and off I go. It is summer. It is a beautiful day. I am a new graduate, and I am leaving campus to meet up with Tem.

So in my head and heart is a sense of completion, camaraderie, anticipation, success, and love! I am of the opinion that no face-lift or nose-job will ever give you this kind of kick!

Feels like being twenty again!

By the time I get to the hotel, the sun has begun to set. Tem is on the veranda, overlooking the ocean, lost in his thoughts, mellow as any man would be on day one of a summer vacation in what we lovingly call Lotus land!

Although I have just completed an important milestone, somehow I feel like I am just beginning something.

Sunday July 24

We leave Sooke's shore to head north on the island toward Tofino. This place is a forgotten paradise, nestled on the west coast of Vancouver Island between strips of rugged terrain, also known as the Pacific Rim. On a good day, if you could see far, you would see Japan. It is the western-most end of our continent.

The shoreline is rugged, primal, secretive, and discreet. The tides roll in and change the scenery every hour of every day while the sunsets wrap you in beauty and awe as you witness the end of yet another day.

And you can't wait for tomorrow to come and start all over again.

Here, and for the rest of the summer, I intend to be truly on vacation. No worries, no concerns, no budget review, no marketing plan, just rest, peace, and the belief that everything will be fine.

At least that is the plan . . . but it is short-lived.

I come across an email I received months ago, and for reasons unknown to me, never read.

So I read it.

My estranged web designer is basically saying that he is done with me and suggests I find someone else to work with. Nothing new there. He mentions a few applications I should be careful with as far as the website is concerned. He has a lot more to say about my attitude, but I will spare me the details! He then recommends I work with someone who knows what he's doing (hinting to the fact that I obviously don't). To be honest, I can't argue with him there.

The light comes on!

This means, someone else can pick up the work from where he left it. So, if we have been unsuccessful at fixing it so far, it is not that it is impossible, but that I have asked the wrong people.

180-degree turn. My website is not doomed after all.

There goes my vacation. Within days, I find someone who is truly talented and hire him to do the job.

And he does.

What caused me agony over most of the summer and ruined many otherwise good night's sleeps, not to mention nice dinners overlooking the Pacific, was fixed in a matter of a few days and a few hundred dollars!

Another precious lesson learned here. My own beliefs create my own limitations. How is that for a punch line? Once I knew it could be done, there was no stopping me until it was done!

What you believe determines what you do.

Sunday July 31

I am daydreaming, sitting on the porch overlooking an inlet on the Sunshine Coast. We have traveled east to the island's other side now, slowly making our way back to the mainland.

This is a favorite spot of ours. Tem and I try to spend a few days here every year. This place is a small community, with quiet roads, fresh oysters, and cold beer all day long if you want. It is sunshine from sunrise to sunset. It is where I think retirement would be a swell thing to do, and that yes, I am ready to sit down and read all those books I have been piling up over the years, starting with *War and Peace*.

Coming to a place where I would agree to put my feet up, unpack, and think, "This could be 'it,'" is a rare event for me, but this place does that, with this man.

But I know that come November, the sunshine will turn into rain, and these fresh oysters will be out of season, and besides, I have read *War and Peace* already, so at this stage, I am thinking it is best to move on.

Wednesday August 3

I am in Vancouver for a few days before heading east to the opposite side of the country. We are going all the way east this time, not even stopping in Montreal. Newfoundland is the ultimate destination.

Although I said I was on vacation and was not going to think, talk, or dream about work, it is hard to resist the temptation. A few calls, a few emails, even a networking event while I am in town. Because, once September comes around, I will officially declare myself off my sabbatical. (I need to start calling it something different because a sabbatical usually comes with a safety net, and this past year had everything but a safety net.) My expectation is to be working and generating an income right away.

Right away, as in sending an email and keeping your BlackBerry on your tabletop because you are expecting a reply. That kind of right away.

I have not been paying attention to those who say there may be a six—to twelve-month lead time to any new clients. I am not that patient. I can't think in such terms.

So I break my rule and engage in some work activities, just enough for me to get a strong lead on a potential contract upon my return.

I also "re-launch" my website with the right picture and some different set-ups.

This time around, it feels different though. For one thing, the magic is gone. You cannot have Christmas in February and think it is just like the real thing. You won't convince me otherwise. Also, I have come to realize that although it might mean the world to me, 99.99

percent of the world will not even know I launched it twice. Hell, they may not even know I have launched it at all. So I guess you can say I have learned to think of it in relative terms.

Somewhat.

Regardless of whether or not it is perfect, or merely good enough, it gives me an incredible sense of accomplishment and relief to know that it is now done. Even though this is officially the second time around, it never felt done before. Now it does.

Thursday August 11

When we get to Newfoundland, more particularly to St. John's, we actually drive to the end of the road, the same one we were on while in Tofino. It travels from one coast of this nation to the other. It is called Highway 1. In St. John's, we can actually stand where the road starts. It was built going west, against the wind, starting, of course, on the East Coast. So we traveled backwards, and today we stand on kilometer 1. Feels like standing on hallowed ground.

What Newfoundland and Tofino have in common are the ruggedness of the scenery, the integrity of its people, and the beauty of its coasts. Tofino is of Native ancestry and culture. Newfoundland is of European Nordic culture. Different. Although they will argue to no end that their salmon is better than the others (Atlantic and Pacific salmon), they have both caught on to the delights of fresh oysters, and honestly, we don't really care who has the best salmon. They are both exquisite to city dwellers such as us!

Monday August 15

We are going nowhere today. Intentionally. We are practicing Tem's biggest lifelong dream: to get behind the wheel of a car and drive into the sunset to wherever the heck we feel like going, and do so for months on end.

So today is a twenty-four hour version of that dream.

We find a most beautiful spot in a secluded bay where we decide to stop for lunch. We have some fruit and sandwiches. There is an old wooden table conveniently resting in high grass between the beach and the road, a road practically not traveled, given the absence of traffic we have witnessed so far.

We are enjoying the silence and peaceful aura of the place when a car pulls in, parks next to our table, and an entire family comes out with pails of fish still trashing about. I am annoyed that they would pick this very spot when this country has over six million square miles of surface, most of it unoccupied. Moreover, this bay is completely empty except for Tem and I.

The family proceeds with cleaning the fish. Fish heads and tails are flying all around us. Seagulls are fighting over this delicatessen, and at the same time, diving in for our sandwiches while the kids are running around our table playing hide-and-seek. I turn around and am about to deliver one of those "Look people" speeches when they walk toward us, hands stretched out in a welcoming gesture, and apologize for the uncleanliness of the place.

Come again?

"Had we known someone would stop here for lunch, we would have cleaned the table and brought a tablecloth."

Oops . . . We are on their property!

Sometimes, life is good to you and it catches you right in time.

We eventually leave the bay and our newfound friends and drive until we come to the road's end. A true statement. We park the car and start on a trail heading to one of the most spectacular places I have had the privilege of seeing, and I have seen a few.

Where we stand is an old tiny cemetery on our left, nestled in the hill, where the most recent tombstones are from many decades ago. People don't come here anymore to lay their dead. The grass covering the path leading to the cemetery is a testimony of a road less traveled. Ahead and all around us is the ocean, the restless Atlantic Ocean, which today is uncharacteristically calm. At our feet is a gathering of stones, conveniently flat, where we can sit comfortably with our backs against the rock while our feet hang over the cliff. A light, soft wind, carrying aromas of sea salt and wild herbs, is the only sound, with the exception of a few seagulls. Even they are quiet. We are looking for puffins, but we can't see any. There are no waves other than the shadows left by the whales waltzing in and out of the water.

We have no idea where we are, and I could not tell you what the name of the place is, and to make it even more surreal, all the pictures I take of the place I later will discover were destroyed due to my high tech agility in transferring them from the camera to the computer. I unknowingly erased them all.

So to this day, this place remains a secret place, almost as surreal as a dream you wake up from. It was, however, a moment in our lives, a place where peace, rest, love, and hope for the future all appeared to be possible. It was also a demonstration that Tem's dream of driving aimlessly is not without its charm.

And we move on only because today needs to yield to tomorrow, and I am getting hungry!

Thursday August 18

Coming back to the vibrant and buzzing city that Montreal is in August, after two weeks in Newfoundland, requires an adjustment. It reminds me of a summer many years ago when the children were still little and we had spent a week in a very rustic cottage, deep in the Laurentian Forest, where the only entertainment was the lake, creeks, frogs, stargazing, and scratching our mosquito bites . . . I say all there was because presumably, with children around, you think of playgrounds, Disney channel, video games etc. We have never been a family to engage in such activities, mostly because I had little time and money for such things, and secretly, because I despised them as well.

The morning we left camp and drove back into the city, we hit the first big town roughly around lunchtime. The children were hungry. Of course, the first place we saw was a fast food chain. After a week of dirt and bug-seasoned home-cooked meals, we thought it would be fun to indulge in your typical burger trio.

It was a busy day that day. After the peacefulness of the woods, this place felt like Best Buy on December 26! It was incredibly noisy, busy, and smelly. We all stood there, somewhat taken by surprise, not knowing how to be.

I looked at my children. They obviously appeared to be out of their element, and that was a good thing to me. A very good thing. I felt secure in the thought that they were grounded and had enough instincts to know what was right for them and that this place was not. So damn proud. I remember as if it were yesterday, standing between a cash register and a garbage bin, smelling of ketchup and cold fries, silenced by the deafening noise of the place, and being happy.

To know that my children will prefer the stillness of nature as opposed to the buzzing of a city somehow means the world to me. Right or wrong, this is what I see today.

Life's moments are not always those you see framed on the wall.

As my vacation draws to an end, so does my sabbatical. The closer I make it to the West Coast, the more I am closing in on my deadline.

There are no hard set rules for when it should end, other than it started on September 6, a year ago, and I always thought it would end no more than twelve months later, mainly because a sabbatical stretching beyond twelve months sounds more like retirement or the unemployment line.

So, as the calendar goes, the year is coming to an end.

Tuesday August 23

Before I draw the line and declare the sabbatical over, there are still a few things I need to do, and in fact, I am sure I could keep finding things to do until such time as they need to wheel me into the old folks home.

Speaking of wheeling me in and out, it is time I pay a visit to my lawyer to review my Will. This time I am prepared to do it. One last item on my "To Do" list. Like most people, I've kept this one for last. My Will is easy: all I have divided by three. That's it. At least you would think that would be easy, but some of my assets are in Quebec, some in British Columbia. My lawyer tells me this current disbursement may cause delay and complications at the time of distribution. This is a polite way to say when I die, it will get messy. I get it.

You should have a Will in each province, my lawyer says. Seriously? He can't be serious. Even I know enough that if you think assets in two provinces can be complicated, try two wills in two provinces! Honestly.

I stick to one will, but I keep for later the discussion around how long I want to lie on a stretcher with tubes sticking out of every orifice of my body when my brain has gone dead. You can only entertain the logistics of your own death for so long without getting edgy!

Friday August 26

Back home. Déjà vu. Now what?

Well, think back to when you were six years old and bedtime was drawing near. You'd do everything to be ignored and to escape the deadline. In the adult world, we usually call this procrastination. Thinking of everything else we could do before we do whatever it is we know we should be doing.

Fear, doubts, wanting to avoid failure at all costs, even if it means potentially losing out on something good, these are some of the factors behind the syndrome of not being quite ready yet.

The well of procrastination is indeed bottomless. There will always be plenty to draw from.

So, as I contemplate going out there and selling myself, I am thinking that perhaps there is a certain level of that going on. Somehow, I don't feel ready. I don't know if I ever will though. I know what it takes to get me to next week, and to the next client, but how to deliver on the whole business plan in a reasonable timeframe and ensure it is sustainable? I need to take care of today and tomorrow, in its most finite minutia, as well as seeing the big picture, being creative, innovative, authentic, calm, cool, and collected.

Holy crap. I used to have a team to take care of all this. Now I need to do it all by myself?

I think I am scared. What if I can't? What if I don't?

One day, years ago, I was a mother of two young children, one of them just a newborn. The New Year was not quite upon us yet, and my husband and I left family and country to travel to a new place where for a whole year, we would live off our savings while he would complete his Master's degree in a specialized field. I did not know what awaited me then, but I sensed it would be difficult. I had always been one up for a new challenge, but that one somehow scared me. At the last minute, when saying my goodbyes while my husband and children were already waiting in the car, I turned to my mother:

"I don't want to go anymore."

She hugged me in silence. I knew she would give me no options. I never really intended not to go. I agreed with her. I was excited about the prospect of a new life, but at that very moment, I was scared and looking for a last minute way out.

So today, I pretty much stand in the same mental place, looking for any excuse to stretch the sabbatical and not face the reality.

But as life would have it, that is not an option.

What helps me pick myself up and get going is a call I get from a friend of mine who is Head of HR in a local company here in Vancouver. Would I be willing to come and speak at a regional round table on the future of HR?

You mean speak as in keynote speaker? Really? And so is launched my public speaking career. More will follow, but this first one sure came easy.

Isn't life a tease? Every time you think of throwing in the towel because things are just too tough, just enough goodness comes your way to keep you going.

PART V

If you want to conquer fear, don't just sit at home and think about it. Go out and get busy.

Dale Carnegie

Today is one year to the day when I came back from Corsica to start my new life. This time, I am back from Newfoundland, and still working at starting my new life. It has been a long new life!

It may be an endless one, like the tides I watched coming and going this summer, never resting. Such is a good life; always new, always fresh.

So I am back in Vancouver, by myself, with no more excuses to delay my new life. It is no longer willing to stand on the doorstep.

So?

Will somebody ring my doorbell? Dial my number? Send me an email? Call for help? Will somebody notice that I am out there, ready, willing, and able to offer a substantial product?

No!

I have come to the absolute end of the road as it relates to getting ready. Now that my course is completed, my website and blog launched, my vacation over, my bank account nearly empty, and luckily, I have secured a few clients, I need to own my new status and establish sustainability and longevity.

Not knowing what my future will be is somewhat of a frightening thing, and it is more so at fifty-six than at any other time in my life, but by now I have had a whole year to get used to it, and yes, I know, nobody can predict the future. However, when one has a nine-to-five job where she is expected to show up every Monday morning, where status reports are reviewed every Thursday, and she knows the amount that will be deposited in her bank account every month and how much she will have at retirement, she has a pretty good idea of what her future holds . . . or at least some of what it holds.

Insecurity is what I am referring to.

In coaching, we like to call this the impossible future. Impossible because that is how it appears. Future because that is what it can be. The name of the game is to make it possible, and that is where I am. Standing in front of that canvas, the mastery will be to transfer these full, impatient, boiling over, can't wait to get going brain activities from my head, moving them past my own doubts and making them work.

Somehow, selling a company felt a lot easier than this! It was part of a team effort. There is comfort in a team. For one thing, the spotlight is not exclusively on you, and failures, like successes, are shared.

Being a one woman band is a lot more drafty than that. It is being live on stage without a crew and no one waiting to drive you home after the show. It's all about you.

Because you know that it takes several hits before you get a win, you believe it is important to cast your net wide. So I thought in the beginning. I have since wised up, but at first, when you start, you think so. You are nervous, insecure, and you feel the need to go big. Bigger than you should, in most cases.

For the longest time, I continue to be a rookie at what I do. Everything is a first and that has its significant share of challenges. I look into social media, networking events, speaking opportunities, board opportunities, contact people at home, abroad, focusing strictly on coaching, and then on HR support, and on leadership development, etc. I inquire about office space, renting meeting rooms, a working visa for the States, creating associations, introducing group coaching. I attend all kinds of seminars online, and in person. I hold so many meetings at Starbucks even my bladder refuses to go there anymore . . . . I meet experts on topics as varied and unpredictable as my moods during PMS: Online learning, emotional intelligence, project management, creating a business online, career transition, not-for-profit initiatives, until such time as nausea and exhaustion are fighting each other to see which will get me down first.

There is such a thing as too much of a good thing.

Pacing yourself is an art. Pacing myself is a mammoth undertaking. Much like the marathon runner, or better yet, like moving into your new house. The need for practicality dictates that you unpack the necessities such as the bed, pillows, kettle, coffee jar, and the cooler holding the beer. Then you put the rest wherever it seems appropriate at the time, and as you take ownership of the house, and actually live in it, you start really fixing it to your liking and comfort.

That is if you are not married to my ex. With him, you need to know where the snow tires are when you go to bed that night even though you are moving in on the 1st of July long weekend. You unpack and store until you drop.

For anyone else, you tend to do it incrementally.

So it is with a business. In the beginning, you need to take care of the basic elements, such as creating a minimal revenue stream (maximal would be nice, but that comes with time), and once that is done, then you need to deal with the long-term, core issues.

The business model I have identified as the most logical according to my instinct, inclination, and desire, is to write, speak, coach.

In that order.

I cannot possibly start by anything else than the book because, honestly, the book occupies 100 percent of my brain space. I am obsessed. Also, the book is where my heart is. Until it is done, there will be no recess.

First the book, then talking about the book, then coaching on the basis of the book's content.

This is my desire. My reality is quite different.

The coaching is what started taking place first, mostly because coaching is tangible, it is what I do, it is what I sell, and it is what people understand.

So I need to adapt.

So I am coaching before I have a chance to finish the book and talk to people about it. Talking about the book was supposed to be my coaching's foundation. Not even started and already it is all mixed up. Promising.

It is probably better that way in the end because, honestly, I still have not resolved the discomfort around my writing. Not the style so much, but the content. There is a lot of struggling in what I say. I don't have a lesson or a conclusion. It is about trials and tribulations. How can I position myself to help others when they see me under that light? I just have an offering, and it is that figuring yourself out is mandatory if you are to be successful at anything, and that aligning with who you truly are, as opposed to whom you would like others to see, takes courage and determination. It is important to know, but few people are interested in finding out this way. So perhaps it is better they know me first; otherwise, they might run.

The other offering I have is: Who you are is good enough. You just need to learn to work with it. You may be different, backwards, unusual, or whatever else makes others uncomfortable, but you are still good. You are not wrong; maybe all you need is a good check-up! Your body needs one periodically, so why wouldn't your mind need it too?

Find your space. Find your voice. And stand for them.

I will not pretend that bliss unfolds miraculously, or that it is a breeze, and or that it doesn't have its excruciating doubting moments. But I will tell you, it is your best alternative to staying in the wrong place.

Inertia will do you in.

Motion will create momentum. You don't need to be smarter than the next guy, have a bulletproof plan, and three years' worth of earnings in the bank. You don't need to have a Ph.D., or be friends with Who's Who in the industry. You just need to be downright driven, stubborn, and determined that you are the best you have to offer. That is where you are going—come rain, hail, or high water. If the next guy can do it, so can you. Might take six months, might take six years; doesn't matter. You're in for the long haul, and no, it is not an all-inclusive, all you can eat and drink scenario. It is grocery shopping for a family of four the day before payday.

It is tight!

So, why go through with this?

Because stretching makes you go further. Who wants to stay put all his life?

And so it is. Like motherhood. Once you've experienced it, there is no going back. It is your new reality. Unlike motherhood, though, you can adjust it, make it more or less intense. My experience with motherhood was that it took some time before I found the control button. I suspect it is the same with much everything else.

Somewhat similarly, the passion you have for what you do will make you put up with the challenges. In the end, it is all the same. If it is worth it for you, then you are willing to stick your neck out and take the punches. If not, you can just pack your goods and move on. You have a choice.

The difficult part is to hold on to the dream while you are working at it, and it is not making itself visible yet. In other words, when the output far outweighs the yield. In financial terms, that is a bad investment. In life, that is a risk. Your tolerance to risk will determine your chances of success.

Not always, but often.

When you start seeing the first glimpse of daylight coming up on the horizon, when once in awhile you have a good day, and you are pumped about what happened, and you feel rewarded, and fulfilled, then you start getting really excited about the potential this holds.

The trick is to get just enough of these glimpses to get you going through the start-up phase. This is where a big chunk of the 80 percent who fail happen to hit a wall.

Hunker down people. This is a ride.

You should also know that unexpected turns of events always happen. Sometimes, they are good and you ride the wave. Other times, they are bad and you roll with the punches. You only hope they are not deadly! Not much you can do about those!

One such surprise for me has been the realization that in working with talented leaders—the definition of my clients—I actually have the privilege of working with smart, witty, sharp-minded individuals who, through our conversations, teach me a lot. Imagine working in a place where every single one of your colleagues is as sharp as a whistle! There is endless energy there for me.

So sometimes, sticking it out takes you places you could have never imagined. That is the magic of resilience.

It is such an extraordinary thing to be part of their lives, albeit for a short period of time, to learn about them and their organizations, to travel into their worlds and get a glimpse of their day-to-day lives. That is beyond nice. It is uplifting. I feel privileged, invited to the head table, special among others, and valuable.

So the surprise is that I actually receive more than I feel I am giving. It is as though I showed up at the cash register with my basket full of goods and the cashier gave me money to take home. How good is that?

Another pleasant surprise is that despite all my efforts to be online and to make myself visible, in the end, it is by word-of-mouth that I start building my clientele. Just like I had thought I would all along.

Had I simply trusted myself and the process, I would have been spared hours of anxiety and unnecessary worries. There is a lot to be said for believing in yourself.

I quickly realize, as I sit with clients, that it invariably always starts with the dynamics within the individual, then with others, and finally, with the organization. For my clients to be successful in what they want to do, we have to find the right starting place, and nine times out of ten, that is right within themselves.

Interesting. This sequence of events strangely resembles what I went through this last year. It seems that the pattern fits all. First, figuring oneself out. In my coaching, working with leaders, I call this self-mastery: the insight on self. Understanding how you are wired; knowing what values, strengths, passion, and needs you have.

Then, figuring out how to offer the best of self and draw the most from life. In the workplace, we call this leveraging. It is impossible to do if you are unable to relate well to others. Finally, it is about putting it all together and making great things happen. We call this superior performance. To me, it all comes down to success and harmony. For driven individuals, one does not happen without the other, not in the long run.

Just like that.

Now, the next big gig for me is social media. I mean in a real and meaningful way. If creating my website was any indication of what lies ahead, then this step will be entertaining to say the least.

But I am prepared to do whatever it takes to bring about success. So, social media it is.

How do you show up as a business on these platforms? Looks to me like they are more fitting for teenagers playing hooky on a sunny afternoon than for a commercial venture. But then again, what do I know? For me, to create my Facebook business page is something I wish I could put off or have someone else do. But true to myself, I do it alone and the thing gets ahead of me. Somehow, I end up with a business page within my personal page, inviting every single contact in my Outlook database, including those I have not talked to in years and those I do not really care to invite. What can I say? That's what I get for not reading the instructions.

Long story short, I end up having to post on my site: "I am sorry, but truly the party is next door, and would you mind all moving to my business page, and leaving my personal page alone, as I really don't intend to entertain anyone here?"

Coaching teaches the virtue of vulnerability. I am so glad I completed the course successfully. At this stage, vulnerability is as familiar to me as milk to coffee. Thinking of vulnerability as just another tool to deal with your day-to-day life is a healthy way to reduce stress. You are who you are and you do your best. That is all there is to it. No apologies required.

PART VI

Act as if what you do makes a difference. It does.

William James

So I thought long and hard about how this whole journey of the sabbatical and the launching of a new career could conclude.

I don't know at this point that I have a punch line, and somehow, I feel like I owe one to my reader. So, for days, I have agonized over how to end this story, and I can't think of a proper ending, other than the proverbial "to be continued."

My sister, who has been reading my blog, following my journey, and listening to my complaints about how to wrap this all up nicely, writes and asks, "Looks to me like you are on your way already; why can't you consider it done by now? What will it take? When will you stop? Or will you ever stop?"

I can answer the last question. I will not stop. This is only the beginning.

However, I just understood something. Being enough and stopping are two different things. Enough has to do with the level of accomplishment, and that is always expandable. Stopping is an event in time. I will work on expansion until I blow up, I suspect. As for stopping, that is not on my radar. I just got started.

The fall is so busy with various trips that I am able to put off finding "the end" to this book for a bit longer. Tem and I are in Halifax when the weather is mild and people are already bracing themselves for yet another brutal winter. Then we are in La Martinique when no one else is there and we can enjoy quiet beaches all to ourselves. Finally, we are in New York, twice actually, when everybody else is there shortly before Christmas when the city is as giggly as a child at the circus. It is true what they say about New Yorkers. They love Christmas.

Even if I had wanted to bring this book to an end, I am not able to. I do not have the last piece, the punch line, the big event. I am looking for fireworks—something memorable. I am looking for it everywhere, expecting it to show up at the least predictable moment. So far, it has not shown up.

It is now Wednesday night. I call Jean-Francois, my firstborn child. He is off to Copenhagen to join his girlfriend, who has been in Europe for the last six months. The time apart from each other has been difficult. Being apart is physically painful when you are in love. Later in life, you realize what a privilege that time when you long for the other is. As he gets ready to leave, he and I clearly understand that he is standing at the doorstep of his new life. When he returns, they will be together, moving in together, seeking new employment, etc. As a mother, I have a sense of "done and delivered." This son is on his way and has been for a while. He agrees.

Suddenly, the doorbell rings. "I need to hang up, dear," and we say goodbye.

The cabinetmaker is bringing back my dresser, dining room, and coffee tables I had sent out for refurnishing a few weeks ago. All this time, my clothes have been on the floor and so have my books. My meals have been a balancing act on my knees.

So today, things are going back to their respective places, and there is a nice cozy feeling to that.

Also, the electrician finally comes in late in the day to connect the new cooktop that has been sitting there, lifeless on the kitchen counter, for over a week. This tells you a lot about my cooking—that I did not even miss it!

The condo seems to fall back on its feet and be comfortable again. Another completion.

Julie calls just as I am sitting down for an apéritif. Perfect timing. She is off to Costa Rica the day after her brother leaves for Copenhagen. She is so excited. It will be a well-deserved break. She has embarked on a very brave and very demanding journey at school. The determined and solid young woman that she is will go places. I know. I have no fear for her, other than the fear of a broken heart. All parents do. But as far as her life is concerned, she sure is on her way.

Philippe, who has lived with me these past few months, has gone back to Montreal this fall. On his way there, he bumped into a renowned chef, who offered him a job in Montreal. This chance came as a surprise to him, and to all of us, since he intended to go back to school. He will have choices to make. Having choices is being rich. This son of mine is the ultimate representative of live and let live! Things happen to him. I think people see in him the talent and depth he carries. This is a son with a brain that will impress you. I know he also will do great things.

All these thoughts have a nice aura of accomplishment for me. They don't, however, take me away from my ultimate goal: finding the perfect place for me to turn the page, and call this period of my life completed, and move on to the next phase.

I am looking for where that line in the sand is. I need an event.

It is not easy to find. It is hard to see big when you look at your own life. When you feel you can do something, or know you have done it, then it does not feel big anymore. It just feels like the normal thing to do. So as accomplishments go, once you have reached them, they are never big. The next gig will be . . . and that is why the line keeps getting pushed out.

So knowing when to stop, look back, and recognize success for what it is, is a gift and a skill.

Under normal circumstances, this is the time of day when I would reach into the fridge, pull out a dish or casserole I would have prepared at one point, heat it up, and have dinner. Of course, no such items are in my fridge. A year has not been long enough for me to go back to cooking. By now, I am pretty sure it will not happen, short of having someone else in the kitchen with me, sharing the labor, the food, and the wine, of course!

Knowing your limitations is also a skill.

Julie's boyfriend, who lives here in Vancouver while she is in Montreal (she indeed takes after her mother!), drops in for a visit. He is off to Costa Rica in a few days. He will be there ahead of her.

"Have you had dinner?" I ask. A stupid question to ask a young man of his stature who can eat dinner on the hour. Of course, he is hungry.

We head out for a favorite restaurant of his in my neighborhood.

What pleasant company he is. What a sound, decent man with values I value! That my daughter would appreciate such a man is comforting to me, regardless of their future.

Surely, my hamster must be having a bad week. Everything seems to be going so smoothly and falling into place.

"What are you up to these days?" he asks. I tell him about all I have done these past few months—my new clients, my blog, my website, my speaking engagement, my prospect in Montreal, my travels . . . .

"Any big plans ahead?" he asks.

"Well, yes; an international coaching association, a new forum group, a gig in Turkey perhaps, and two new clients in Vancouver, and, of course, this year will be the book of the year . . . . Uh, I mean, the year of the book!"

He pauses, looks at me, and smiles. "No. I like the way you said it. The book of the year sounds about right!"

We laugh.

Then there is silence.

And then it dawns on me.

Why not draw the line here?

A casual conversation on a Wednesday night on Denman Street, when it would appear that life has taken back its normal course.

Normal is certainly a line as far as this last year goes.

EPILOGUE

I write this epilogue with the words of Sinatra's famous song, "My Way," in mind . . . . Doing it all alone is overrated, but doing it my way was the right thing to do, because in the end, it is what is real.

You often think of landmarks in your life as events that will change it. Such as your graduation from university, your marriage, your first real job, that promotion you wanted, etc., only to realize that you are the same the day after. The earth did not move, and the skies did not open up, and you still have to put a load in the washing machine and stop by the ATM to get some cash. Romance isn't what we make it out to be.

So it is with reinventing your life. I was trying to fit the events on a timeline and draw the line from when I started to when it would end, but I am finding that my business, my life, and everything else that is organic, is incremental, one small move at a time. There is no drop dead date. There is no start or end date; just a series of events adding up to a life.

And that is how it goes. When you think about it, I am pretty sure the Middle Ages did not end on a Wednesday night either. There must have been some kind of overlap before the world declared that it was now in the Renaissance . . . so, looking for a line somewhere does not really make sense.

Surely, I have some unfinished business that will stretch into the next month and the next year, but this journey I embarked on over a year ago has now become my life, and I could not tell you when it happened.

It just gradually did, building outwardly.

If I have learned anything, it is that often life is not where you go looking for it. That is why you must be willing to go places you would not normally choose to go. I am a firm believer in the strategy of slicing the elephant to eat it one slice at a time. Trying to start a journey with the end in mind is at times overwhelming.

You should know that to start with well-defined marketing and business plans totally makes sense, and it definitely will contribute to your success. Make no mistake. All the work you put into preparing the journey upstream will benefit you downstream. That is a sure fact.

But there is something else you should know.

If you don't have all you feel you need, and don't know all you think you should know, that is no reason not to start. If you know enough to know that you are not where you want to be, then, start moving in another direction. Don't wait until you have all the answers.

If you don't know what direction to move toward, start moving in any direction.

Go.

Try.

Experiment. Turn every rock, find your compass, your passion, what makes you shiver, what keeps you awake, what you would do if you had all the time in the world, all the talent you want, and all the money you need. Keep looking until you find it. This journey is about finding you and what you can make of this life. It's definitely out there.

No point waiting for an epiphany, a new job, or the lottery. It is not a milestone. It is but a pebble hitting the surface of the lake, changing how it looks, one ripple at a time, and that is quite all right. There is time.

It is a journey, remember? Once you embark on it, you are already where you should be. The rest is just homework.

The only expectation you can truly have is to face the unexpected, and the only conviction you need is that you will be perfectly capable to deal with what comes your way. You have what it takes.

It is possible. So much is possible.

Gisele Aubin Executive Coaching

In this age of overnight success stories and the silver bullet solution everyone is looking for, Gisele Aubin offers a refreshing approach. No one is born a hero; nor does anyone become one overnight. Whether admitted or not, everyone struggles on the way, learns by trials and tribulations, and a great many of us fear more than we let it be known. However, everyone is capable of success. If you have any doubts, reach out to Gisele Aubin and ask her.

You can reach her in many ways:

www.giseleaubin.com
www.facebook.com/gisele.aubin.executive.coaching
www.twitter.com/GiseleAubin
coaching@giseleaubin.com